WHAT HAPPENS IN GROUPS

R. D. HINSHELWOOD

WHAT HAPPENS IN GROUPS

Psychoanalysis, the Individual and the Community

FREE ASSOCIATION BOOKS / LONDON

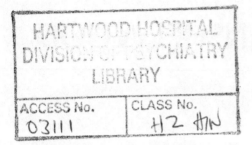
Published in Great Britain in 1987
Free Association Books Ltd
57 Warren Street, London W1P 5PA

Copyright © R.D. Hinshelwood 1987

A CIP record for this book is available from
the British Library

ISBN 0 946960 89 5

Impression: 99   9 8 7 6 5

Printed in the EC

This book is dedicated to the small community of Stephen and Louise and Emily and Nell, whose growth and development have also had something to do with me.

Contents

List of examples

List of figures

Preface

I have aimed at two things: to establish a way of thinking about groups, communities and institutions in general, and therapeutic ones in particular; and to point to a direction in which the specific practice of therapeutic groups and communities might develop.

Work with groups of any kind is a peculiarly hybrid occupation. I once wrote:

> *Psychologists, sociologists and biologists sit with their backs to each other. And in the middle of this uncomfortable three-way see-saw are doctors and therapists trying to keep their balance. This is the acrobatic position we work in in a therapeutic community. It is the glorious privilege of academics to know that they are on the track of knowing everything. It is the humble gloom of the practitioner to know that nearly everything remains uncertain and paradoxical.* (Hinshelwood, 1983a, p. 167)

Mostly, therapeutic work with people emphasizes the psychological aspect. Even working with people in groups emphasizes the psychology of individuals and groups. Group therapy usually starts with an understanding of individual psychology and moves towards the group. Then, perhaps in order to understand the larger group, communities and institutions, we look to the experience of smaller groups. In this book I have moved in the opposite direction.

My work with groups took place first of all in the larger group of the therapeutic community, and only subsequently did this become informed by my learning of individual psychology during my own psychoanalytic training. I would claim that this book tends to redress the balance, with more of a binocular view of the individual and the social dimensions. I have not found it necessary to separate experiences in small groups from those in large groups, which is the currently acceptable view. And I believe that what is discernible in the large group is relevant to the small group. The experiences in the two kinds of groups are certainly different, but in my view this is because the small group hides certain aspects of people together – rather than because the large group is an inherently different kind of collection of people. In this I support de Mare's contention that our real need is for more research into the larger group and not into small groups (de Mare, 1985). My approach is, however, rather different from his since he repudiates the idea of sub-grouping and multi-group systems altogether in pursuit of the group-as-a-whole large group. My view is to accept the fact of sub-groupings and understand the needs and defences bound up in that phenomenon.

I would argue that it is commonly neglected that all small therapeutic groups, however carefully managed in a select private practice, are nevertheless part of a multi-group system – certainly in the phantasy life of the members and the therapist.

Coming at groups from the social perspective does demand a sturdy willingness to suspend some of the comforting frameworks that have been evolved for thinking about small groups. This is all to the good, if somewhat uncomfortable and insecure. What it does mean is that one is exposed to the lack of rigour in formulating large group experiences and processes, as Millard has recently demonstrated and is himself trying to remedy (Millard, 1986). The latter part of this book is itself an attempt to move towards more rigorous systematic thinking about the types of groups and communities and their therapeutic or anti-therapeutic properties.

The social–personal interface

Poised between a realization of the powerful forces at play in the institution and the need to act effectively on the individuals, the therapeutic community is right at the interface of the social and the personal. It is not possible to think about therapeutic communities, and what understanding of people in groups they offer us, without acknowledging Tom Main, the originator of the term. One of his later reflections, recalled from his time as a war psychiatrist, is that some social systems seem to be more healthy for the individuals in them than others:

> *Psychiatrists working with units in the field were all aware of certain battalions in which individual breakdown was common and of others in which it was rare ... In the field one met well-run units of high group morale which carried significant numbers of men with manifest personal breakdown who refused to report sick, and who would soldier on effectively; and other units which combined to make an unhappy and inefficient whole with generalised reactive miseries, complaints, delinquencies and psychosomatic disturbances, even among men with records of stable personal health ... What was it about battalions which made the difference in promoting or failing to promote the health of the individuals within them? It had nothing to do with the social structure ... Nor had it to do with the role relations; these too were also laid down ... It seemed to be something both more vague and more important than these; it was the culture, the human folkways by which the systems were operated, the quality of human relations inside the social structure.*
>
> (Main, 1977; reprinted in Pines, 1983, pp. 200-1)

The quality of the human relations and the overall social functioning are clearly connected in some way. It is this kind of observation that I have investigated further. Social relations can affect mental health, some kinds can be therapeutic and some anti-therapeutic. What is the difference? How can we begin to look at the culture, the 'human folkways' by which the system is worked?

A central tenet of therapeutic community work is that responsibility is located in the right place. It has clearly been understood that responsibility can be misplaced. A coherent recognition of the psychodynamics of responsibility within the group is the hallmark of all successful therapeutic communities, and they embody a consistent push towards sharing responsibility, deriving 'from the

15

staff's readiness to offer patients and staff reciprocal adult roles with participant powers and responsibilities' (Main, in Kreeger, 1975, p. 60). In most therapeutic institutions responsibility, together with the resources and power needed to meet it, comes to be relocated in the staff by common social agreement; and irresponsibility, together with the attendant sense of depletion and helplessness, accumulates in the patients/residents, also by common agreement, so that 'only roles of health or illness are on offer; staff to be only healthy, knowledgeable, kind, powerful and active, and patients to be only ill, suffering, ignorant, passive, obedient and grateful' (p. 61).

Part I of this book begins to look at this kind of social reallocation of human resources, qualities and responsibilities. Chapter 4 describes some of the dimensions of the internal world of individuals which are relevant to their functioning in the (to them) external world of the community in this way.

The therapeutic community and the defensive community

Main argues that this socially agreed redistribution of human qualities and responsibilities is a normal process in large groups and thus in helping institutions – and that it wrecks their helpfulness. He relates it to projection and introjection, as dynamics at the interpersonal level. These represent defence mechanisms which can then be understood in terms of anxiety and unconscious phantasy. His clearest example is that of a neurotic marriage:

> *A wife for instance may force her husband to own feared and unwanted aggressive and dominating aspects of herself and will then fear and respect him. He in turn may come to feel aggressive and dominating towards her, not only because of his resources but of hers which are forced into him. But more; for reasons of his own he may despise and disown certain timid aspects of his personality and by projective identification force these into his wife and despise her accordingly. She may thus be left not only with timid unaggressive parts of herself but having in addition to contain his. Certain pairs come to live in such locked systems, dominated by mutual projective fantasies with each not truly married to a person, but rather to unwanted, split off and*

projected parts of themselves. Both the husband, dominant and cruel, and the wife, stupidly timid and respectful, may be miserably unhappy with themselves and with each other, yet such marriages although turbulent are stable, because each partner needs the other for pathological narcissistic purposes.

(Main, 1975, p. 58)

The rest of part II (chapters 5-7) are concerned with the group manifestations of projection, introjection, identification and idealization (chapter 5); the implication of the individual's own unconscious internal world in the interpersonal relations of the community (chapter 6), and the implications of this interpenetration of the personal into the social for the overall features of the community, of its regime (chapter 7).

To explore and exemplify these themes it was necessary to rely heavily on the work of others. In particular I derived a great deal of help from Elliott Jaques, who first discovered the concept of the social defence system, and his co-worker Isobel Menzies. They elaborated the idea that the social system itself can come to be used by the members to provide a psychological protection from personal suffering (chapter 5). It is this defensive manipulation of the work and of the task of the institution that is manifest in the cultural phenomena that Main refers to as 'the "human folkways" by which the system is operated'.

Personal experiencing in institutional work

This book has come from a prolonged personal acquaintance with a therapeutic institution. The observations are those of a participant, not a distanced observer. The hope is that they will therefore strike home with familiarity to others who are also buried in the work of an institution.

However, the book has been written with an emphasis on the experiences that people have, the experiences both of those in work and, since this is a therapeutic institution, of those who seek therapeutic benefit. Human experiences and human relationships form the bedrock of the structure and also the energy of institutions. I have used psychoanalysis as the most searching of tools that exist at present for

understanding human experience. I have avoided a simplistic trans-
position of individual psychology into the communal arena. Instead it
is important to recognize that the events occurring in collections of
individuals are not merely aggregates or summations of the individual
events. There is a true separation of level in the object of study. I
have tried to understand the experience of the individual in the
communal, rather than to study a psychology of the community. The
book starts from its grounding in painful human experiences which
are the stock in trade of the therapeutic community, including the
peculiarly typical experience of the meetings that feel wrong.

The chapters in part III formalize many of the kinds of
experience met with in therapeutic community work, and especially
the problem of the sense of failure at the individual level, and that of
morale at the group or institutional level. The experience that staff,
either as individuals or as a group, have in relation with the patients is
as important as their informed and knowledgeable observations made
from an emotional distance. Their experience is to be had and used,
rather than denied and projected.

The character and pathology of institutions

The work reported in this book lends itself to being a guide to finding
one's way emotionally around institutions in general. The community, although dealt with in its own terms, reflects the experiences
and phenomena that confront one in any institution. It is not just a
background to treatment but an actual ingredient which may be used
to avoid the benefits of treatment through throwing up defences, as
with the transference neurosis in an individual psychoanalysis. It is
therefore important to go beyond simple description of the life of a
community and to develop a framework for thinking about the nature
of institutions that could be applied at least to the therapeutic
community.

Part IV is a further formalization of the material, which starts
with an especial interest in the functioning of boundaries, particularly
within the community. The malfunctioning of boundaries is a clue to
the site of projective escape from experience. In these chapters a
beginning is made to define important dimensions of the institution,
those which make up the community personality. These are: fragility,
rigidity, flexibility, and the degree of disturbance at any one moment.

Therapeutic community practice

The work in therapeutic communities has a particular objective: to enable individuals to change in themselves. This work has a dialectical quality since consciously it is focussed in communal events, but at the same time it is focussed towards individual objectives.

Part V comes back to this special objective of the therapeutic community, and explores the qualities needed in the community personality to make it a vehicle for a therapy of the individual (see chapter 18). If that is conceived in the most general way as an enhanced ability to face experiences that have hitherto been defended against, then the community can be seen as a containing 'mother' to be projected into, and to be re-introjected for purposes of supporting a containing function within the individual (see chapter 19). The dimensions of the community personality described in chapter 17 actually turn out to be those that define certain kinds of container of disturbance.

The boundaries of the community need constant maintenance to preserve their flexibility. The working out of the organization for this maintenance work is, in itself, the challenge each community faces, as it is the challenge for each individual to maintain his or her own flexible boundaries.

These ideas need to be operationalized into a form of practice for the therapeutic community worker through giving an extended example (see chapter 20) and some didactic guidelines (see chapter 21). Finally, chapter 22 brings us round full circle by putting the findings reported here back into the context of the small group again, and showing their relevance to group therapy practice.

The original outline for this project was given as a talk to the staff at the Marlborough Day Hospital in 1971 (Hinshelwood, 1972) and a later report of some conclusions appeared as several chapters in *Therapeutic Communities: Reflections and Progress* (Hinshelwood and Manning, eds, 1979), published three years after I left the hospital. I have talked about the material contained in this book on many occasions, and frequently at the annual Anglo-Dutch Workshops on therapeutic communities (The Windsor Conference).

The particular community I worked in is, alas, no more, having died in 1977. The demise of the work that we put so much into has added considerably to the arduous quality of digesting the experiences and learning that came from my time there. The result is a view on the nature of institutions that derives from an intimate involvement in one, and the attempt at a rigorous use of a therapeutic framework (a psychoanalytic one) at the social level. One of the illustrations has previously been published in a different form (Hinshelwood, 1985).

This has been a difficult book to write over far too long a period. Although I have written it, and although the particular frame of reference I used was not fully shared by all of the team at the Marlborough, the work derives from the collective intuitions and shared experiences of the whole team, comprising many people – some of whom outlived the seven years that I did, and many of whom 'passed through' for shorter periods. It is difficult to single out individuals, but I have to mention Sheena Grunberg and Roger Hobdell for their enlivening contribution and competitiveness, and Angela Foster, Anna Christian, Hazel-Anne Lewis and Patsy Hall for their softer support and their tolerance of the many anxious moments we all went through.

Finally I want to acknowledge the delicate editorial touch of Bob Young in his helpful suggestions and encouragement; and also the meticulous work of Sara Beardsworth in getting my manuscript into fit condition for the typesetter to set and the reader to read.

I have kept the term 'patient' even though it may have prejudicial connotations. I have done so on the basis that, (i) the hopeful use of alternative terms, such as members or residents is often disappointing and the prejudices reappear, and, (ii) in fact the thrust of the argument in this book is that unrealistic prejudices should not be merely dismissed but learned from. It is hoped that the examples and the analysis of them will clarify what the term 'patient' means at different times, and where its traditional and prejudicial meanings come from.

I have also tended to keep to the masculine version of the third person in order to avoid clumsy phraseology; and also because the views expressed in this book indicate that matters of prejudice are not adequately dealt with by a simple manipulation of terms.

PART I

Raw experience

1

Suffering the experience

Because, like many others, I was naive and innocent when I started work in a community, I was very often affronted in the early days by how uncomfortable the work was. It seemed wrong for a form of therapy which I had thought promised satisfaction for everyone. The first impact the community makes on the newcomer is usually to do with the way it makes him feel. This chapter will therefore start with some views about experiencing the community.

Group meetings are not always useful events. Also – and this is very different – groups are quite often experienced as useless. I shall distinguish between groups that are really useless and those that feel useless. To do so I shall start with the latter. The argument put forward here is that whatever the experience, it can be put to use even if it is the experience of being useless.

Meetings which go wrong

What I have in mind here is the kind of group in which nothing appears to succeed. The staff end up feeling cornered and at a loss. When a meeting seems to go so wrong despite the concerted efforts of the staff, there is often an attempt to discharge the disagreeable experience in the post-meeting staff group.

Certain features appear in these discussions: first, a somewhat tense and ultimately fruitless discussion about the purpose of community meetings; and then the staff's emotional release of complaints about the meeting as having been bad or wrong. These staff discussions follow a predictable course. Some people will question the worth of the meetings, often quoting perplexed patients who are confused about their purpose. Others, perhaps having been identified with the community longer than most, regard the matter as long settled and barely worth discussing any more. These discussions are always inconclusive and lead to no change. No-one can give convincing responses to the doubts, and at the same time no-one presses them to a conclusion. The result is never an answer, or a new resolve, or a decision.

Central to these discussions is the atmosphere of the meeting. It comes from a common experience that something did not feel right about the community meeting. The staff have collectively experienced a discomforting event. And then they get it off their chest together. Their different individual responses – whether dismissive criticism or resigned faith – are put, as staff believe they should be, into rational terms; but they have resulted from the shared feelings. The discussion is a release of disagreeable feelings rather than work at defining the problems.

We can now move on to consider the kind of community meeting that gives rise to uncomfortable staff.

E 1.1 The meeting that went wrong*

This meeting of some thirty-five people took place on a Tuesday afternoon some three weeks before the Easter break. There were three visitors to the meeting and one new patient. The preceding week in the community had been marked by several explosions of violence (normally very rare in this community).

Shortly after the appointed time for the start, we settled into an uncomfortable silence. One or two people came in late filling up the empty chairs. The last of the late-comers, Adam, moved to a chair but found the bottom of it broken. He hesitated, uncertain what to do because there were no other free

---

*All names used in the illustrations are fictitious.

chairs, except that Brian, sitting just by where Adam stood, was occupying a second chair with his feet. Brian made no move to help Adam, nor to offer to move his feet. Eventually Christine, a woman on the opposite side of the room, asked Brian why he did not offer Adam his second chair. Brian then moved his feet off the chair without a word. This example of silent unhelpfulness displayed the mood of the meeting very accurately. The silence closed in again. After some five to ten minutes a patient, Diana, began to speak and uttered a monologue addressed to no-one in particular. She seemed set to continue indefinitely, and the introspective and monotonous style of her monologue seemed well adapted to the unresponsive nature of the meeting on this particular day. Her talking formed the major activity. She made a number of points, but the most emphatic and most often repeated message was that she was utterly inconsolable. The meeting had been posed the problem of consoling the unconsolable.

This characteristic leaden atmosphere weighed heavily against the possibility of taking up any work that might be presented to the meeting. Diana might have been challenging us to console her and be defeated in the attempt. Eventually a member of staff, Noel, said that nobody, it seemed, was going to get help from the meeting today. There was no immediate response to this, but later an interpretation, also from Noel, provoked a final expression of indignation and hostility. More than one member of the meeting complained that they were suffering under criticism and discipline from the staff. It was as if Noel had been a callous task-master whipping the patients to work.

This group culture, consisting of sullen and unresponsive patients passively resisting tyrannical criticism by the staff, is a very common feature of 'the meeting that goes wrong'. The staff ended up unhappy and disconcerted that their patience in tolerating Diana for so long was so cruelly unrewarded.

The meeting moved towards a 'paranoid' confrontation between patients and staff, from which the staff at least needed to extricate themselves afterwards. They had involuntarily been categorized as criticial, demanding and impatient. When Noel expressed his feeling that something was going wrong, was he actually being bloody-minded? Or had it unlocked something in the meeting? What had happened? How might Noel have used his feelings differently?

An alternative intervention

The following example is in contrast to the last one.

E 1.2 A successful interpretation

On the Friday of the same week the community met in the afternoon. The atmosphere was unpromisingly identical to Tuesday's meeting, and it had persisted throughout the week. After a prolonged silence, Ann began a somewhat ugly argument with Nancy, a member of staff. This was the expression of a difference of opinion that was many weeks old and this instalment might have been designed to confirm that the quarrel remained unchanged and Nancy unforgiven. The rest of the meeting sat unresponsive and bored.

Another member of staff, Owen, cut through this with the remark that it seemed nobody felt like working today, and that we would all rather be out enjoying the sun. An unhappy discussion then ensued about loving someone you cannot trust. Many more people contributed. The mood had shifted away from sullenness towards sadness and participation.

This intervention on Owen's part was at first glance very similar to Noel's on Tuesday. However it was puzzlingly successful. It produced a significant shift in the meeting quite different from Tuesday's. There was the same reference to his own feelings that something was wrong – there seemed to be no work going on. What was the difference? Perhaps Owen's intervention in the second meeting carried with it the recognition of difficulty, perhaps he visibly understood the longing for warmth that was felt at a very basic level. On this occasion the intervention was largely received as toleration of misery and inability; whereas on Tuesday it had seemed like criticism of irresponsibility. An element of compassion and consolation, combined with the acknowledgement of failure, had forced its late entry into the previous scenes of accusations and condemnations.

Attitudes about the staff grow up in these meetings, quite often without foundation. Yet their unreality is itself a reality. It is my purpose to try to understand these mysterious developments in the culture of the meetings.

Is the therapist's personal experience his own?

All the puzzlement and inexperience revealed in these hit-and-miss interpretations must be familiar to others who, like me, came to therapeutic communities rather green. The aim of the chapters that follow is to move towards surer judgements of these situations and of the 'interpretations' that might be used, and above all towards the staff member's surer grasp and use of his own experience while he is undergoing it.

What was Noel's experience in the first of these meetings? If he felt fed up with the group, might that not have told him something about the meeting he was in that day? If so what could he do about it? These are questions which this book will address. They will form the basis for a methodology of work in communities.

Explaining experience away

The point of view taken in this book is that the therapist's experience is his own. It belongs to him. Yet he may distance himself in various ways from that experience. As I noted at the beginning, there is no shortage of reasons that can be thought up to explain what happened. However, these reasons are often a therapist's way of coping with his experience of the moment. Easily found reasons are so often disappointingly superficial ones. They give rational weight to the therapist's wish to discount, dismiss or ridicule his own disagreeable experiences.

Most therapists, and inexperienced ones especially, can be pushed to elaborate on what exactly was good (or bad) for their group members, and why this should be so (it is much less easy for them to say why it was good or bad for themselves). It may be that some particularly silent patient has spoken at last. Or that there was a general air of euphoria about. But beyond the therapist's immediate intuition of himself, there lies in his feeling a clue to the life of the group and the people in it.

A patient's silence needs to be seen as a communication. The therapist's irritation (or pity) has a meaning to be discovered and learned from. It is not necessarily therapeutic that the patient speaks for the first time without it being understood what his previous silence had meant. A gloomy meeting might also be a communication – if so of what? It is for the therapist to facilitate the discovery of the meaning.

The experience of good or bad in the group is an important clue to the dynamics of that group. Yet, so often a therapist will seek simply to have a good group experience with his group members, and to minimize the bad ones.

The efforts of the staff after the meeting that goes wrong, described at the beginning of this chapter, are efforts to abolish the disagreeable experience they have just been through.

The therapist's effort

It is important to recognize these needs of the therapist at the outset. The job of discovering the group and the need to express oneself in the group do not sit happily together. All therapists, at all times, struggle with this.

The therapist can regard almost anything as valid material. This should include even his own discrimination between good and bad. The therapist's effort to understand the group is itself part of the group, and may affect the group. Many sensitive neurotics can discover and exploit their therapist's feelings (especially his unknown ones). Generally a whole group will look, from the beginning, for what the therapist wants of his group, what he judges to be a good one, and what he judges to be bad. Like all other members, the therapist may give quite clear, though unconscious, signs that he thinks the group should behave in certain ways, and is uncomfortable or upset when it doesn't meet these expectations.

The therapeutic community is unusually difficult for the therapists. Traditionally, psychotherapeutic freedom is limited to free verbal association. However, the therapeutic community is a form of psychotherapy that also requires a maximum degree of practical freedom. But this is not just verbal free association. The community lives together. All sorts of non-verbal communications get tied up with all sorts of activities, behaviour, organization, working and decision-making. The counterpart to free association is the principle of permissiveness. Alongside this, however, is the need to keep reasonably good order in the community. A dilemma arises here for the staff member. He has managerial responsibility for the amount of dirt on the kitchen floor and may indeed be revolted at standards that are far worse than one would normally be willing to tolerate. However, at the same time he must balance this against the conditions that therapy demands. The permissiveness that allows dirt on the kitchen floor cannot be allowed to override standards of hygiene. This is the experience a member of staff must frequently suffer. Yet it is just this experience which then becomes an opportunity for therapeutic work.

The therapeutic community worker cannot simply choose one or other side – managerial or psychotherapeutic – managing the community or managing experiences. The worker's allegiance is demanded by both. In this book I hope I shall be able to show from my experience the potential use of this dilemma.

Summary

Two initial examples have been given of groping attempts to make therapeutic interventions in community meetings. The ways in which these are experienced by members of the community have shown up as radically different in spite of their content being very similar. The experience of the community by the members was introduced as the primary focus of attention. It has been suggested that the staff member's instrument for his work is his own experience, and that the specific use of his own experience is the professional skill the staff member must acquire.

2

Understanding in action

Large groups have large problems. In spite of this, school assemblies, military parades, annual general meetings, shareholders meetings – all exist for explicit purposes. They tend, however, simply to confirm that this body of people exists, instead of harnessing their skills in actual work efforts. The powerful forces released in large groups reinforce the status quo. In the therapeutic community this may add up to giving permission for psychological symptoms and complaints.

Characteristically the attempts to perform rational work in the large group are hampered by the emotional force of being a member of a large group. As a vehicle for the community to organize itself, decide for itself and examine itself, the community meeting obviously has much working against it. The very forces that bring about the cohesion of the community also seem to hamper sensible work. It is of some interest why this should be so. Khaleelee and Miller (1985) have started a project to try to tap these processes in the largest of all groups, society itself.

Running the meeting

In many communities the meeting is the central forum in which to organize the work of the community. To fulfil this function, the meeting usually has a high degree of formality and is clearly structured. Roles such as chairperson and secretary are assigned and there are committees to draw up agendas and to administer decisions. Even with this vigorous structure these meetings often lack actual vigour. Decisions may take an interminable time to make, and there may be a low level of or perfunctory involvement from a large proportion of the members.

In the community I am describing we had come to a different arrangement. There were separate 'business' meetings, so the daily community meeting functioned less in a business sense and more as a window on to the community dynamics of the moment. It was therefore a window on to the ways in which the business might be interfered with. Following Crocket (1966) and Tollinton (1969) we adopted the assumption that better decisions might be made if the 'community neurosis' were somehow elucidated and contained on its own, and that better personal treatment might be given if neurotic involvement could be released from the community as a whole. We assumed, too, that neurotic intrusions needed examination, and that the examination should be free of value judgements and political debate.

Action and words

In chapter 1 a meeting was reported in which some process led the community into a state that felt wrong. That was contrasted with another meeting in which the outcome felt a lot more satisfactory. The different outcomes suggest a spread along some dimension (Fig. 2.1). If the initial state is thought of as undifferentiated, the interventions seemed to provoke differentiation into one of two alternatives. The first was to bring about an unpleasant hostile situation in which antagonism and distrust flew between staff and patients. The second outcome was not a display of hostility but a verbal expression of the unhappy state.

This is an important dimension in the development of a community discussion. At one end an unwilled display is enacted in the actual relationships in the meeting; and at the other there is a conscious verbalization. I shall use the term 'dramatization' for the enacted display. In the state of dramatization, members participate in the 'drama' without a conscious decision to do so. They simply find

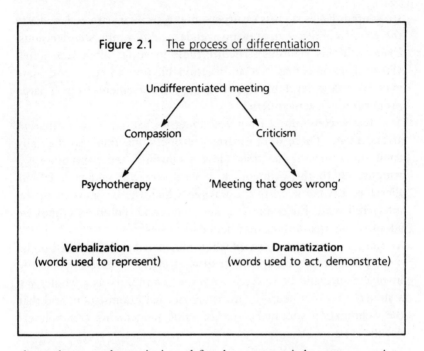

Figure 2.1 The process of differentiation

Undifferentiated meeting

Compassion   Criticism

Psychotherapy   'Meeting that goes wrong'

Verbalization ———————————— **Dramatization**
(words used to represent)   (words used to act, demonstrate)

themselves caught up in it and for the moment it becomes convinc-
ingly real. It would seem best, as in other forms of psychotherapy, to
aim for the verbal, conscious end of the dimension. But so often it is all
too easy for patients and staff to get caught up in the dramatizing
process. As one is being carried away, as the staff member in the first
example found, it becomes impossible to extricate oneself. In that
example the staff member had ingenuously stated his own feelings that
no-one was working. At that moment he became implicated in a
dramatization – hostile patients confronted by menacing staff.

Dramatization does not mean psychodrama. An awareness of
being caught up in the drama is usually lost. The drama is unwilled
and, since it is unconscious, one does not have the choice to get out.
This is not psychodrama, although psychodramatic techniques could
help to bring the community towards the verbalizing end of the
dimension (for instance, see the resolution by psychodrama of an
intractable fire-setting problem in Hinshelwood and Grunberg 1975;
see also Ploeger 1981).

Anzieu (1984), in an attempt to relate psychoanalytic theories to
groups, has chosen the notion of phantasy as basic to group life:
'Certain more recent observations show that the group situation is

perceived essentially in terms of the most archaic phantasies' (p. 117); and he discerns certain specific kinds of phantasies which are central to group life. In this view the group holds a phantasy, and involves a collective regression to phantasy activity on the part of all the members. In contrast, the view I am presenting emphasizes the group as the object of the individual's phantasies, with a subsequent negotiation of these individual tendencies in the arena of the public space. I will therefore use the term dramatization because it is the public form of individual phantasy activity – phantasy in action, but negotiated in public.

We will now go a little further into exploring the varieties and twists that these dramatizations take.

Mutation of hostilities

When hostility is dramatized in the community meeting, it takes a variety of forms which are linked up with one another. Typically a 'tyrant' is driven further and further to compel his resistant underlings

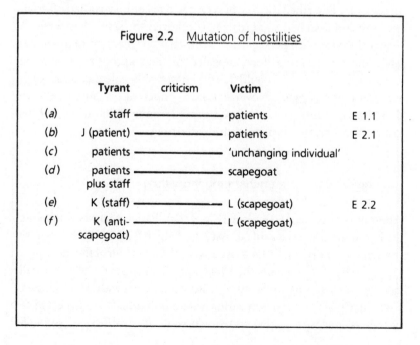

Figure 2.2   Mutation of hostilities

	Tyrant	criticism	Victim	
(a)	staff	——————	patients	E 1.1
(b)	J (patient)	——————	patients	E 2.1
(c)	patients	——————	'unchanging individual'	
(d)	patients plus staff	——————	scapegoat	
(e)	K (staff)	——————	L (scapegoat)	E 2.2
(f)	K (anti-scapegoat)	——————	L (scapegoat)	

to co-operate. In the first example given in chapter 1 this was simply dramatized as the staff criticizing the patients. Figure 2.2,*a* shows this process and how it is related to a series of dramatizations.

E 2.1 The NCO

In a silent unresponsive group a hitherto passive man, Bill, emerging from a psychotic breakdown began to complain of the cleaning duties which he was doing without the assistance of other patients. In the context of the meeting he became thereby identified with a tyrannical role. His complaints escalated to include a recommendation for a militaristic organization of authority and responsibility, taking for himself an 'NCO' role (Fig. 2.2,*b*). He now looked to the staff to support his accusations against other patients. The more enraged he became the more he identified himself with the staff as authority, releasing in himself a more and more excited state which resembled hypomania and persisted, in fact, for some weeks thereafter.

In the event described the role of tyrant had become separated off from the staff and assigned to a patient. It relieved the staff: they were no longer the tyrannical persecutors. Yet then it put them into a dilemma, since the tyrannical patient appealed to their authority in a quite unrealistic way. They could hardly support his demand for such tyrannical government. Nevertheless, to undercut his support was to drive him into total isolation and further tyrannical domination. This is a no-win situation typical of dramatizations.

Inversions – the unchanging individual

Another change may take place (Fig. 2.2,*c*). Patients can avoid feeling criticized for their lack of activity or help by directing a hostility towards one individual who is occupying the attention of the meeting – and wasting it. Criticisms then focus on this member – whom I will call 'the unchanging individual'. The unchanging individual holds a particular place in an organization where individuals are expected to change themselves. If that individual is at all capable of a paranoid mode of adjustment, the meeting goes into a spiralling hostility while that individual attempts to defend himself. In this instance it is not the tyrannical side which has become located in one individual, it is the victim that has been identified in an individual.

The scapegoat is helplessly prodded towards the centre of the stage as the person standing out against, and wasting the help offered. It is understandable that members of the staff, too, may be strongly tempted to join in this kind of criticism and believe they are fighting for the aims of the community. We will come across this ingredient in many more examples in this book. Scapegoating in which one individual carries all the criticism and blame for the waste of the opportunities (Fig. 2.2,d), can reach levels where it becomes an institution within the community. Ill-defined phrases such as 'unable to use the group' become standard and may become automatic justification for disciplinary sanctions or discharge – literally sending the scapegoat, laden with the sin, out into the wilderness (see, for example, E 10.1, 'The reign of terror'; and E 16.1, 'The bureaucratic constitution').

From the perspective of a dramatization we see just how much the scapegoat's 'sins' really belong to the whole group. That is, responsibility, blame, criticism and tyranny are issues for all or most of the members contributing silently or dramatically to the process.

The anti-scapegoat

Another variation arises when a tyrannical sense of responsibility is located in a member of staff who becomes embroiled in the hostilities. When he recognizes the futility of pursuing the unchanging individual and attempts to turn the discussion into more fruitful channels, he is confronted by a problem. He becomes the staff's tyranny personified (Fig. 2.2,e).

E 2.2 The anti-scapegoat

Oliver, a member of staff, was moved to confess that he had been angered by an unchanging individual to the point where he felt like telling her to shut up. He said all this very carefully and explained that he had not actually told her to shut up as he did not wish to hurt her. Although this was spoken with great care and considerable humanity, it became clear only a few minutes later that she was now convinced that she had been told to shut up by Oliver. And somewhat later Oliver was even rebuked for being unkind by another staff member.

The unfortunate situation (Fig. 2.2,f) was that Oliver had not just become the mouthpiece for the responsible staff, but had become completely isolated and discredited as the hostility itself of the whole meeting. This was a 'valuable service' which the meeting was willing to encourage him to keep. Even the staff left him high and dry. It is similar to the scapegoat but works in the opposite direction, so to speak. Instead of having all the blame dumped on him, he became the inhuman judge assigning all the blame. We might call it 'anti-scapegoating' – of a discredited judge.

The meeting had reverted somewhat to the original form of hostilities. Patients were inhumanly criticized by staff. However it is here more elaborated – specific individuals were identified, the judge and the scapegoat were personalized, and others (staff as well as patients) took the reassuring opportunity to be comfortable onlookers whose only function was to keep the actors in role. For the individual member of staff, like the patient, this is one of the most unpleasant experiences he is likely to come across in community meetings.

The unfolding process

Figures 2.1 and 2.2 serve as charts to locate the kinds of experiences in the meeting that goes wrong. To summarize, the process of differentiation unfolds under the direction of two principles:- (i) the process becomes increasingly located within individuals eventually producing a scapegoat culprit and other personalized roles; and (ii) the content of the quarrels becomes increasingly specific. Overtly or covertly it centres around the achievement of change, and becomes more and more specifically related to inability, defect, helplessness and the refusal to change or 'be different'. Doubt is cast on the ability of the community to do its job. The individuals lose themselves to become personalized elements as the whole meeting dramatizes something going wrong.

In the more successful interpretation (E 1.2) the staff member used his experience of the meeting to do two things – to regret the lack of work, and to identify with the member's wish to be warm and comfortable. So the intervention grasped the experiences of both sides of the potential dramatization – the regret, and the wish for reassurance. We shall see later on the importance of this kind of bridging intervention.

Summary

The unpredicted responses to the hit-or-miss efforts described in the previous chapter have a sense of their own. The responses are to be seen as enactments of relationships between roles – dramatizations. The staff member attempting to understand must place himself in the context of this action in such a way that he does not go along with it or deny his place in it. These dramatized relationships have a complex and fiercely trapping quality of their own. They unfold into great detail and ensnare unsuspecting members of the meeting, staff and patient alike.

3

Resources for unconscious dramatization

I shall now give some material from a sequence of three community meetings. The potential for a constantly unfolding process of dramatization is very varied in a community of people who know each other well. At the start of the event described in E 3.1 the community was shocked by an announcement which caused despair about the treatment of mental illness.

Enacted relationships

The shocking news with which the meeting began elicited a considerable amount of disturbance in the community. The staff, as we shall see, were as shocked as the patients and took several meetings to recover. It is a striking observation that the first impact of the news was to mobilize a hitherto silent 'schizophrenic' who uttered a very disturbed comment. The example shows how the struggle with disturbance was dramatized in the form of an enacted 'relationship with disturbance'. Later the particular form of the relationship changed.

E 3.1 The suffering community

At the start of the first meeting it was announced that one of the members of staff, Pauline, was suffering from depression and had been admitted to a mental hospital for treatment.

Pauline had frequently been absent from work recently and there had been various excuses. The response to the announcement was mixed. There was a minimal expression of guilt and sorrow and some anger at the previous deceptions.

Somewhat incongruously Chris, a patient, was angry that Pauline had once laughed at Dave, another patient. A member of staff, Queenie, asked Chris more about his feelings. He said, quite seriously, that he was a Sioux Indian last century who had been killed and become manifest again in 1942. This remark was not easily comprehended. Some people needed to have it repeated by others who had heard what Chris had said. He subsequently interpreted this himself by saying he felt lost. This was more understandable. The meeting attempted somewhat half-heartedly to go into his difficulties about feeling lost and isolated. But there was an air of despair implicit in this sense of being lost.

During the first part of the discussion about Chris, Eve entered the room late, and sat on the chair next to Chris. Eve, in a manic, domineering manner, began to join in, alternately distracting attention from and contributing to the theme. She asked Chris if she could tell the meeting what they had discussed privately together. He agreed perfunctorily and she told us he had said he had not had a woman for eight years and had masturbated ever since. At this point, Eve then complained that Fran, sitting on the other side of Eve, was scratching herself. A moment later Eve stood up and moved to the other side of the room saying she could not stand the noise of scratching and she sat on the arm of Gary's chair. She continued to ask Chris about his sexual habits amid increasing embarrassment. The effect of all this was to move the attention on to Eve, and Chris was becoming eclipsed again. In fact this was the first meeting in which he had spoken.

When the meeting was jolted by the news of Pauline's depression the capacity of the meeting itself to handle madness became subject to doubt. The meeting investigated the problem in the dramatizing mode. In these exceptional circumstances Chris had come to the fore. He had offered himself in the maddest way as the most immediate opportunity to express the despair. Chris had actually said in his schizophrenic way that he felt brought to life again ('made manifest') after a long time – at least until Eve arrived in the meeting.

Chris was made manifest again because he was the opportunity for the exploration of madness. His position in the meeting could be seen as expressing the various views or relationships with madness. These included (i) its incomprehensibility, (ii) its embarrassment and alienating effect, (iii) the fear of it, and (iv) the entirely isolated, individual quality of it (as masturbation).

The dramatic use of Eve

The meeting continued in an interesting way. The use of an individual to express some of the common fear went on. But the issues about madness changed and a new individual expressing the new dramatization came to the fore.

Some people became acutely aware that Chris was becoming neglected (reminiscent of Pauline's inaccessibility and the community's helplessness).

Now the problem for the meeting was how to handle Eve. As we shall see this became a new dramatization of the despair about handling madness. Eve told the meeting of the various names she had used, each connected with different aspects of her life. She emptied her handbag and demonstrated each of its contents. This manic domination was becoming an increasing problem, at the same time representing the insoluble madness.

Through the mode of dramatization the problem was being stated in various ways: (i) how well did the community treat madness? (Pauline had to go to another hospital); (ii) how could others in the community be protected from the eclipsing quality of madness? (Eve eclipsed poor Chris); and (iii) how did the community cope with madness in so far as it is very intimate and internal (Eve's embarrassing revelations about Chris's sexual life; and indeed her own revelation of the contents of her handbag and her identities)?

The problems provoked by Eve's actions also threw into relief the despair of the community, the feeling of impotence and powerlessness, or alternatively the inability to contain Eve's personality as her hand-bag contained her belongings. The temptation was to retreat into 'masturbation' fantasy.

None of these questions and despairing answers were verbalized. Because they were being dramatized through the relationships in the meeting, they could only be known through an intuition, through the experience of being in the meeting and in its relationships. Only by placing oneself in the dramatizations going on could one feel the impact of the news. It had been hustled out of sight.

In the long run that did not spare the agony. Doubts about the community were still deeply felt even though they were not accurately located and confronted.

Despair dominated the further progress of the meeting. As Eve became an increasing problem, attitudes in the meeting hardened, she was spoken to more and more sharply and attempts were made to shut her up. She reacted by becoming more tense, easily distracted and dominating. The meeting helplessly drifted around the problem. She focused the dramatization of a despairing but ineffective helper.

The meeting ended overwhelmed by the experience of the distressing news. But the experience remained lost in the dramatized roles and relationships. However, things never remain the same. Although we shall see, as the example goes on, that it is not easy to follow the changes as they happen.

Mutation

The second meeting, on the following day, opened with some silence, and then Harriet (a patient) began a rambling complaint about the difficulties of getting a job after a breakdown. She was deriding a social worker for encouraging her to apply for something an ex-patient would not be acceptable for. The theme of the meeting turned to the doctor's role which was supposed to smooth things with future employers, and to decide for patients what their work should be. Staff member Richard picked up this retreat into an orthodox medical model and suggested that there was a wish for an infallible doctor who could make everything right for patients, and moreover that this was an attempt to grapple with the problem of Pauline who had had a breakdown herself, and of whether she would ever be fit again for the work of caring for patients in the way they felt they needed.

There was little response to this interpretation and the discussion about Harriet's job rumbled on in a desultory way. At about this point Eve came in, late again. She sat by the door reading a newspaper. After a while she made a comment about the tedium of Harriet's problem. Reliably the meeting turned again towards Eve. Harriet fell silent in a satisfied disgruntlement that presented her as a sorrowful unfortunate who has the right to expect better than she is getting. Her pointed self-exclusion could be taken as the expression of being neglected in favour of someone less deserving (not only Eve, but also Pauline who had been thrust to the fore again by Richard's interpretation).

This was rather different from the previous meeting. Harriet's view of things seemed to represent today's mood more accurately than Richard's interpretation. He had reflected on the meeting of the day before but, as the mood had changed overnight, the interpretation was not therefore relevant and was not taken up. Now the mood was no longer a straightforward fear of madness and despair. Today it was a self-involved disgruntlement at the intrusion of someone else's disablement or inadequacy. The staff's inadequacy was dramatized especially by the non-response to Richard. The feeling of being displaced was clearly dramatized in Eve's entrance and Harriet's triumphal eclipse.

There had been no effective interpretation to grasp the mood verbally. The meeting then split into two. Some patients stood against Eve's mad dominance, trying to stop her. It was an attempt to make up for inadequate staff who were not doing their job of controlling madness.

Others encouraged Eve to talk and disrupt. They represented a hostile indignation at the staff's inadequacy and the patient's lost rights. They expressed it by using Eve to attack and disrupt the 'staff's' community meeting. Towards the end of the meeting, some members of staff began to bring about a verbal expression of the anger, dramatized through the medium of Eve's disruptiveness, which they interpreted as a conflict over the value of the community.

The detailed significance of this splitting in the group process is important and will be examined in chapter 17. The largely subterranean movements set in motion by the news at the beginning of the week had begun to surface towards the end of the second meeting when some of the staff had been able to verbalize and face the depth of hostility and disgruntlement.

Verbalization

The third meeting represented further dynamics around this situation. The community was brought a step nearer the verbal end of the dimension and towards a more realistic discussion.

This third meeting opened with silence that was eventually broken when Sarah, another member of staff, entered slightly late. Ian remarked on the dramatic entrance into the room which, he said, was worthy of an actor. Now Ian actually was an actor by profession, who had just been admitted to the hospital. Richard remarked on this and suggested that Ian was trying to let the community know about his own entrance to the community. Ian then set off on a long account about his mother who was a burden to him and emotionally blackmailed him.

This led to a discussion mainly between Ian and another patient, Jane, about the longing to make friends and the need or otherwise for company. The discussion drifted on to the problem of work and then to the guilt about not working. Ken, another patient, denied this sense of guilt and brought in a complaint about unjustified accusations (which was his mode of dealing with guilty self-accusation).

This discussion was trying to grasp the hopelessness about getting on with any workmanlike activity here and now. But the meeting was poised to descend into the familiar persecuting criticism, avoided on this occasion by successful interpretation.

Crippled parents and the crippled relationship

A staff member drew attention to a particular visitor who was in the meeting that day. He was a doctor who was applying for a vacant consultant's post in the hospital. It was pointed out in connection with the discussion about work that this applicant was visiting because he wanted to work here.

Some brief attention was given to the visitor now. But another patient, Laurrie, objected that the theme of the meeting had been lost. The lost theme – which, however, was still actually around – was the working relationship with a sick doctor. Any working relationship between patients and staff was especially difficult to acknowledge. This was elaborated in a series of interpretations by Richard and Sarah, who were visibly working well together. They verbalized the current experience of the hospital as a burden. It consisted of the sick doctor Pauline, like Ian's burdensome blackmailing mother, and the vacant consultant's post as a neglectful and absent father-figure.

Material from the previous meeting and from earlier ones was brought into the discussion which now broadened out to include many more people. The problem of Harriet's job was reworked in a more lively way, and then the problem of whether to conceal or confront breakdown and madness. Eventually the meeting got back to consider the anomalous position that Pauline would have in the hospital when she returned after her breakdown, being now half-patient and half-staff. In the context of the meeting she embodied a living relationship between staff and patient or between healthy and unhealthy parts of the same person.

Part of the improved morale, and of the ability to begin to look at the very alarming situation, was due to the fact that a benign circle was operating. The ability of the staff to work together towards the end of the second meeting put heart into the community, which eventually responded. This in turn put heart into the staff again. The meeting finally began to use words in a more open working over of the meanings of the news about Pauline.

In this instance, the use of interpretation to expose certain personal phantasies about parental relationships was relevant only in so far as it touched the actually enacted dramatization of a relationship there and then in the meeting.

Summary

The community had shown its impressive resources for dramatization. Between Chris, Eve and the rest of the community a whole range of attitudes and relationships with madness were played out in the dramatizing mode in the first meeting. Chris was somehow drawn in from his personal exile in total silence, to manifest the madness. Then Eve took over more assertively as the personification of uncontrollable aspects of being mad.

The second meeting had shifted as Harriet came forward to personify a new dramatization. She represented a shift towards a confirmed bitterness that sat as an impervious cloak around her. In the end, by linking with the attitudes of the whole community, a corner of the cloak could be lifted. This development was then taken over into the third meeting.

Most impressive of all, perhaps, was that third meeting. At this point the action was taken by a newcomer – it is not without interest that he was an actor. Through the dialogue with Jane, his entrance was moulded to fit the community's need to discuss its present burdens and its despair at the imagined state of the hospital.

Roles assigned in the dramatized relationships are very varied and changeable. In a group of people there are impressive resources for recruitment to these roles. The example in this chapter describes many different individuals being brought into play as they became in turn the most suited people to play out the required attitudes and relationships of the moment.

PART II

The individual's own community

4

The internal community

The community is a collection of individual minds. In part II, I propose to begin tackling the difficult problem of the place of the individual mind in the community. So far I have been considering features of the community as a whole. Now I shall go back to the individual's own experience. In order to do this I have drawn on the discoveries of psychoanalysis. I shall begin by distinguishing the 'internal world' of the individual from the 'external' world of the community.

The unconscious and the transference relationship

There are two key psychoanalytic concepts – the unconscious and transference. The 'unconscious' is a specific entity. Though unknown by the person himself it retains a dynamic influence on his life, his development and the significant relationships that he makes with people. It is not just a psycho–dustbin, a repository for mental waste. Its contents are highly active in the deepest aspects of his life – but he does not know about them. The idea of the unconscious is both difficult to grasp and also commonplace. Because of the radically changed view of human beings since Freud, the idea that there is an influence operating in a person's life without him knowing about it is familiar, yet to get an idea of what that influence might be in a personal sense is difficult.

Dreams are one route into this, and from the beginning of the human race there has been interest in dreams as embodying some sort of knowledge that is not consciously known, often knowledge about the future. In contrast, Freud showed that there was indeed unconscious knowledge, that this was in the form of memories from the past, and that they were memories of extremely painful experiences, feelings or impulses from childhood. In the dream these memories are highly disguised and confused with present occurrences in the daily life of the dreamer. However, Freud showed that there is a latent meaning to be found in each dream, which comes from the unconscious pain of the past.

These painful memories not only come back in a disguised form in dreams, but they also emerge unwittingly in the person's everyday life, his attitudes, relationships, preferences and prejudices, and in psychological symptoms.

When the unconscious intrudes into the current life situation it causes 'transference'. This is an inappropriate relationship full of inappropriate feelings which distort rational and conscious motives and thought. These intrusions are quite unconscious – that is their hallmark. However, the person will forcefully argue their conscious reasonableness. Post-hypnotic suggestion is an exact experimental model of the unconscious. A subject responds, without knowing why, to suggestions which his hypnotist has placed in his mind when in the trance.

A transference relationship would be an appropriate relationship at another time and with another person. It is usually a relationship from another developmental age – some time in childhood – and with a parent.

When a person enters analysis he comes to use the analyst as an 'object' that he can place in a variety of positions and roles which suit his own personality. The analyst fits, as it were, into a template by means of which the patient examines the people in his world. The analyst does little to disturb this process except by putting it into words. When analysts started to analyse children they used toys, and noticed the toys were positioned and put in relation to each other. The use of these toys corresponded closely to the way adult patients place their analyst into positions and relationships.

Transference intrusions into the community

I am arguing that the way in which people in communities and in community meetings place each other in roles and relationships corresponds exactly to the unconscious positioning of 'objects' in adult or child psychoanalysis. My suggestion of the intrusion of emotional dramatizations into community meetings therefore corresponds exactly to the notion of transference intrusions in the psychoanalytic setting. Dramatization is transference at the community level.

Through these three concepts – the unconscious, the transference and dramatization – the individual and the community can be related.

External and internal worlds interweave

Freud (1914) described two forms of recall of the personal past: (i) a conscious memory which can be put into words; and (ii) a reliving of the past – an unconscious compulsion to repeat patterns of relationships.

The past is lived now through these 'old' relationships which live on inside the person's mind. They are akin to phantasies, though unconscious ones, and they constitute a mysterious inner world of the human mind – the past that has not been left behind.

The unconscious script

The notion of a troubled relationship hidden away inside the individual is enormously powerful in understanding life in the community. The unconscious phantasy relationships of a persecuting, hostile and suspicious kind, as discovered by psychoanalysis, compare with the community dramatizations described above, especially those in chapter 2. In the following examples the external world of the community is seen in the light of the internal world of the individual.

E 4.1 **The persecuted victim**

In a community meeting Ellen changed from being a leader of a practical discussion on hospital organization to become the sad victim of an unwarranted attack which had happened the previous night. At the time she was staying in the small in-patient unit, and she had come back for supper with two men who were day patients, not resident in the unit. The day patients were not entitled to supper and Ellen was 'attacked' by the night nurse in charge of the unit.

Apparently she was told off again by Susan, the nurse who was in charge the following morning. Susan, who was present at the meeting, gave a less harsh version of the occurrence.

It seems that Ellen had not in fact known these regulations since she had been living in the unit for only two days. Ellen took on the role of innocent victim unjustly condemned. She cried and cried and implored Susan not to criticize her so. For Susan, it had been necessary to explain the supper regulations to Ellen. Yet everything Susan said, Ellen took as searing criticism and responded to with wounded crying.

The meeting gained momentum faced with Ellen's tortured responses. A righteous indignation against the night nurse now developed. She was pictured as neurotically unfit for her job. Ellen remained tearfully hurt and it appeared nearly impossible to focus attention on her own role in all this.

Had she in some masochistic way attracted an attack upon herself? She was indeed at the moment suffering under what she believed were continuing attacks from Susan. Ellen skilfully countered any attempt to look into her own potential for fitting into a victim role – cowering away from the group into her tears, as if the meeting was pursuing the same attack. Eventually a crisply impatient member actually 'gratified' Ellen by taking up the role of harsh inquisitor, and the meeting polarized for or against her.

Ellen felt a chillingly vicious attack of blame and condemnation. It was however quite remote from other people's experience of what had gone on. Ellen's version came from her own internal world of experience, in which she was prone to writhe under the flagellation of an internal persecution. Externalizing this conscience neutralized it by discrediting it.

The world of actual external relations often provides very convincing justifications. The example shows how an internal 'bad conscience' was cloaked by enrolling external participants. The internal sources of such situations were then denied, and the external provocations acknowledged in order to gain external support to discredit the persecutor.

This does not deny that she could, at times, adapt well to the external world of the community. At this very meeting she had effectively led a discussion about important community issues. Her leadership potential also enabled her to dramatize her own internal relationship (the accusatory persecution) in the arena of the external relationships in the meeting.

At the end of the example given, Ellen clearly came to be tormented by an actual cruel critic in the external world of the meeting, but this became a screen for hiding a script written by her unconscious internal world.

Being unconscious, these very powerful influences are only experienced with the mystifying aura of a dream or with the haunting quality of irrational and undefinable moods. Relationships with internal 'objects' (like Ellen's persecutor) are powerful sources of anxieties that dwarf those based on external reality.

The neglected external world

In the next example, the patient could not tackle the pressing issues in her external relations with her son because she was too caught up playing out her own internal relationship in the external world. Again it is a demolishing, blaming conscience which persecuted her for her failure as a mother.

E 4.2 A mother's remorse

Esther came into the Friday meeting towards its end. She was quite upset and this was obvious. Her face was puckered like a child about to cry. The attention turned immediately to her. Her son aged seven was going to start at a residential school the coming weekend because Esther was not able to care for him. While she had been attending the hospital, her son had been staying with her sister. Esther had been to see him this morning and when she arrived her sister had been hitting him in anger. It turned out that this was because he had been taken to the dentist but had refused to have his teeth done (in the past he had undergone many operations in hospital for webbing of the vocal cords). Esther had taken him back to the dentist herself and they had managed to hold him down against his struggles. When back with her sister, Esther had come under attack for her son's bad behaviour: her sister put it down to Esther's bad mothering. This had gone on to an argument about whether or not Esther should go with her son to the school on Sunday. The sister was against it. Esther complained bitterly about the criticism of her mothering. She had subsequently met a friend, and as she told us of this her distress mounted. A similar argument had ensued with the friend, who had also criticized Esther's mothering and advised against her going with the son on Sunday. Esther was particularly aggrieved because this friend was also a psychiatric patient who had similarly come to grief as a mother.

The meeting was at first interested, becoming increasingly sympathetic to Esther and eventually outraged and angry on her behalf. The repeated pattern of cruel criticism was too much. The meeting offered advice on how to retaliate and how to defend her rights with her son. However, Esther seemed impervious to the advice, unable to consider any practical steps for Sunday. As she continued, the meeting became more and more indignant towards her sister and her friend, and left aside the problem of the son's needs of his mother.

In this instance Esther remained enfolded in her hurt relationship with a cruel accuser who had become embodied first in the sister and then in the friend. She forgot the grave issue of her son's needs when going away to school for the first time. The external world was left to look after itself while Esther was absorbed with the pain of her accusations and persecutions. Being so absorbed in her internal hurt she in fact further neglected her son. It is important to see that, although Esther appeared to be acting and relating to the external world (her sister, her friend and the meeting), she did so only as it touched her internal pain and her self-accusation.

The other reality of internal relations

The upshot of using the external world to dramatize the internal is the denial of the existence of the internal world, and at the same time neglect of the external world.

Internal relations give a special and personal quality to the external ones. An infatuation with a lover is a poetic mystery. Its unreality often becomes rapidly apparent. Children's terrors in the night have a wholly internal source.

With similar illustrations, Swenson (1986) makes the same point about disturbed patients on an in-patient psychotherapy ward, one of whom 'was attempting to impose her internal world upon the external world of human relations ... to enact a master-slave relationship with the nurse ... In the second case the patient was enacting the relationship between the beaten, abused, ridiculed poor girl in person and the smug, sadistic, sarcastic keeper of the keys' (p. 158).

An internal world of powerful emotional currents works like a distorting mirror through which the external world is glimpsed without any recognition of the internal influences. It is a world of very active influences, a barely conscious landscape of specially loved or hated figures (known to psychoanalysts as good or bad 'objects'). These figures, such as Esther's conscience, are experienced unconsciously as totally real and, in the examples, cloud any vision of the actual challenge of the external relations.

These 'objects' are the stuff of dreams and phantasies which dwell on various acts done to, with or by these internal objects. The object is held inside the person and kept safe or expelled; or it intrudes itself, or slips away; or it suffers, or retaliates. It can be injured or damaged; it can die or fragment and leave behind some remains that act as constant reminders of an irretrievable loss.

The 'good object'

There are phantasies which concern an object which can bestow a sense of goodness, radiance or power that is felt to be contained inside oneself. Its loss would amount to a complete personal breakdown, the bottom dropping out of the world. The condition of one's whole being and life and body is felt to be caught up in the vicissitudes of these phantasies about the 'good object' inside. If this wonderful object is lost, dies or fragments, the whole world inside feels dead or fragmented; and then the world outside is permeated by such a vision as well. 'The suffering community' (see above, E 3.1) discovered that it had a sick doctor, which provoked internal crises of psychotic degree. The community represented a world that had broken down when one of its special 'objects' had been lost.

The 'bad object'

There are other phantasies in which a specially 'bad object' is roaming the world inside. It takes the form sometimes of a belief that the body contains a disease, a cancer or a pain. Or it may be conceived as a very cruel conscience. The bad object is felt to have the single-minded aim of hurting and destroying. There are then terrible fears that the person, or his wonderful good object, will be harmed, killed, mutilated or fragmented by the bad one.

Psychoanalysts have meticulously portrayed these grim convictions with which patients live, and which then hang gloomily over the community. Anything in the community which resembles these evil phantasies rapidly triggers off the personal gloom and pessimism.

The community of experience

For its members the community is itself a personal world of experience. Individual nightmares are played out in the community arena. Internal security, as well as external, depends heavily on the condition of the community itself. A community that seems damaged, lost or fragmented, triggers off just those same fears about insecure 'internal objects'. Ellen's cruel criticizer suddenly reared up in the form of the nurses in the in-patient unit. The community had now become in reality, like her internal world inside her body, a place where an evil thing endangered her.

At other times there is anxiety about the community itself when it is perceived as the 'good object' of the internal reality. In E 2.1 ('The NCO'), Bill felt an escalating need to keep the community tidy, clean and in good order. He feared the encroaching 'bad objects' in the form of other patients who were making the community dirty and untidy. Bill then had to retrieve himself and the group from a desperate situation single-handed.

Omnipotence

In this case Bill turned to the first place he knew, the staff, for help in his mammoth task. It was a task grown mammoth because that was the size of the internal phantasy which was operating. The size problem is important. Although distressing phantasies occur in everybody, some people are intensely prone to oversized anxieties. These come from the belief that the internal world is endangered in a specially powerful way. The task of putting right something so damaged may seem equally enormous, and the person feels helpless. This helplessness is itself profoundly multiplied by the feeling of having lost the omnipotent (good) object that could have sustained him. There are then a number of attitudes that can be adopted to mitigate the sense of impotence. One is to deny any responsibility and assume an apathetic state in which someone else is responsible; another is to turn the feeling of impotence into a drama of accusations which completely discredits the accuser and therefore the person's own irresponsibility. The largeness of the task is also accentuated by the largeness of the actual group.

It is because this task seems so far beyond him that the patient looks for help. Yet if he secretly believes the task is beyond human abilities altogether -- and most patients do – then it is only some omnipotent thing or person that can tackle the impossible-seeming task. He therefore seeks an omnipotent community. He demands what the myth of the community as paradise (E 5.4) seems to offer.

The therapeutic community is not omnipotent – although at times exaggerated claims may be put forward for it. No doubt such claims stem directly from the need to believe one exists (just like the claims at times for the most improbable physical treatments in psychiatry). If something omnipotent did not exist, then – like God – it would have to be invented.

No community can pass itself off for any length of time as being as effective as the members need it to be. It can only dash these hopes in the end. Despair and fears about holding themselves together come back to patients at the drop of a hat. They inevitably do so in the therapeutic community.

Persecution and guilt

I have concentrated on the despair which has brought patients to look for help. It results from phantasies about destructive objects and feelings; and they are connected with phantasies of the loss, death or fragmentation of the 'good object'. Anger, hatred and envy also occur, but in my view they are attributed to the patients by members of staff too often; and by patients to each other or to the staff. Despair may not be recognized often enough.

There are reasons why despair is not clearly recognized or spoken about, while anger is over-emphasized. When a patient causes a member of staff to feel despair it means making him suffer something painful. Quite often, that staff member will perceive the patient as actively causing hurt and will interpret it as a result of a wish to hurt. What was once despair comes to be seen as an act of hostility. Such a misperception invariably calls forth a counter-hostility, perhaps very intensely. The patient then feels misunderstood, or feels that the staff member, like himself, cannot stand the despair. He suddenly feels let down. These two people are then set on an escalating train of events, as illustrated in chapters 1 and 2.

It is true that a dark aggression lies at the root of these phantasies of despair within. However, the staff are called first to understand the despair being communicated by the patient at that moment. The staff are expected to feel the despair because the patient feels it (is often forced to feel it through being coerced into a dramatization). He must start in the right place where his personal feelings are.

This said, it is important to move on to consider the underlying aggressive phantasies. There are two particular forms of internal aggressive relationships with objects. They may, as we have seen, appear as external once they are dramatized under the leadership of a particular person and under the shadow of a particular community event.

1. Paranoid-schizoid position

The first form is a highly paranoid state in which there is a terror that some evil presence (which may be inside the person, or outside), is motivated to hurt, attack, fragment or destroy the person. Such phantasies make their appearance in everyday life in the milder form of prejudices, unaccountable irritations, and sometimes in frank mental disorders such as psychotic delusions of conspiracies. If the 'bad' object is thought of as inside the person, it may be conceived of as some death-dealing illness – cancer is a common representation of this – since the reality gives a convenient hook for this kind of phantasy. This persecutory anxiety, in its primitiveness, should be regarded as the earliest form of painful experience in the life of human beings from birth onwards. The maturing of the individual involves a progressive modification of these phantasies towards realistic appreciations of actual dangers in the world.

2. Depressive position

The second form of aggressive object-relationship is characterized by sadness or guilt. In this case the 'bad' object is believed to be motivated to hurt, damage, kill or fragment the 'good' object (or loved person). The person fears for the object/person he loves, as if his life depended on that object. The fears for the good object supplant fears for the self. The pining for the good object, that may be injured or dead, gives rise to profound feelings of responsibility for the condition of the loved one, and this forms the core of a sense of guilt and remorse. In turn, it leads to strong urges to repair the damage, or to restore life, often with a sense of hopelessness.

These two forms of object-relationships consist of specific phantasies of aggression – one leading to fear for oneself, the other a fear for the loved one (the 'good' object). Persecution or guilt arise from these two different configurations of the self in an aggressive relation to his 'bad' objects. They are known as positions – *the paranoid-schizoid position* and *the depressive position,* as named by Melanie Klein (see Segal, 1973).

The second of these positions (the depressive), with its characteristic feeling tone of guilt and responsibility, arrives later in the development of the human infant, and is ultimately the basis, through the urges to repair, of the human struggle towards constructive efforts of love, devotion and duty. Typically in the course of development, and frequently all through life, there is a significant admixture of persecution and guilt, giving rise to what is felt as the more punitive and crucifying experiences of guilt. The experience of something damaged is then mixed with a damaging punishment of the person himself. Although these two positions are clearly distinguished, in practice there is a spectrum of experiences from pure paranoid fear, through fear of horrendous punishment, to guilt that can be atoned for.

Ellen and Bill

Ellen (see E 4.1, 'The persecuted victim') illustrates a fear for the self – that is the paranoid-schizoid relationship. Bill (see E 2.1, 'The NCO') on the other hand, illustrates a fear for the good object, the community.

I have pointed out that a member of staff can easily feel attacked when the patient is actually trying to convey despair. The staff member is momentarily thrown into a paranoid-schizoid relationship. External reality was internally twisted by phantasy. Since the patient caused the staff member pain, he was perceived as a cruel object that was motivated to cause the pain. Unfortunately this ready sense of persecution is not at all unfamiliar and can be brought out easily in 'normal' people. Patients experience these phantasies with a maddening intensity. The experience feels despairingly inescapable and uncontrollable.

It will be understood that a community which exists to confront painful things will frequently be experienced as an evilly motivated object that is out to cause that pain for cruel reasons. Some part of the community may be separated out as that 'bad object', as in the case both of Ellen and of Bill.

Retaliatory self-defence may then create the spectacle of the loved community under vicious attack from some hurt member. At this point others will have, as an exquisitely sad phantasy, a poignant sense of their community being damaged or killed. That will then lead to either heroic or despairing efforts to protect it.

An ineffective community

Powerful feelings exist about a community whose ability to function is in doubt. It may be felt to be going down under cruel, damaging attacks. This sense of a failing community is far removed from the hoped-for omnipotence. The community which should love, cherish and restore will seem to be crippled. The source of such damaging attacks is often discussed in terms of the external world. Most members will be sensitive to criticisms of the community – too dirty, too disorganized, too expensive ... outsiders such as administrators from the National Health Service may appear overzealously ready to doubt the value of therapeutic communities. To a major degree, this is an externalization of the internal relations of the members.

Sometimes a particularly pernicious situation arises. Projections of the kind described can actually fit the external authorities. In that case both community and outsider work out, unconsciously, the demise of the community – a truly fateful dramatization (Baron, 1984). And the members are blinded to their internal relations by the 'convenient' external ones.

Reparation

Out of sadness or guilt there may spring other phantasies, which lead to action attempting to protect and put the community to rights. Again, repairing the community is an externalization – based on the hidden internal phantasy of repairing the internal world and its objects.

Activities carried out externally may succeed, in spite of the despair. They then have a real chance of forming the basis of an introjection that will construct a repaired object inside the internal worlds of the members.

When this reparative effort does not withstand the demands for omnipotence and comes to be revealed as ordinary and limited, then other phantasies arise. Despair grinds further into the pores of the community. Depressive defences may arise, as with Harriet's role in the example of the suffering community (E 3.1). Retreat into a mournful apathetic self-pity draws attention to the suffering of the self – in order to distract attention from a suffering good object (the community). Guilt and responsibility can then be temporarily evaded.

Fragmentation

Fears about the destructive effects on one's self or on the precious object often take the form of a belief that the object has been fragmented. The completeness of the annihilation makes repair seem an impossible task. Despair takes on a specially tenacious quality. The gravity of this kind of phantasy process, and its relevance to the more seriously disturbed patients that accumulate in a therapeutic community, are indicated in the following passage:

> *the anxiety of being destroyed remains active. It seems to me in
> keeping with the lack of cohesiveness that under the pressure of
> this threat the ego tends to fall to pieces. This falling to pieces
> appears to underlie states of disintegration in schizophrenia ...
> the early ego splits the object and the relation to it in an active
> way, and this may imply some active splitting of the ego itself ...
> I suggest that the primary anxiety of being annihilated by a
> destructive force within, with the ego's specific response of falling
> to pieces or splitting itself, may be extremely important in all
> schizophrenic processes.*   (Klein, 1946, p.5)

This is taken from a seminal paper that introduced the importance of
splitting processes in disturbed personalities. Work with groups
appears to suggest that these processes are even more apparent in the
dynamics of groups of disturbed personalities, and that group
membership brings a particular susceptibility to feeling 'annihilated
by a destructive force within'.

A great deal of evidence will be gathered in the course of this
book to suggest that the fear of annihilation by fragmenting is central
to life in a community and to feelings about it which touch on the
internal phantasies about one's self.

Summary

The defences described above are collectively operated but relate to
the personal experiences of the people operating them. The
psychoanalysis of individuals has discovered certain kinds of 'primitive' phantasies at the root of the human personality which give rise
to unrealistic anxieties, terror and guilt. Such phantasies appear to be
especially visible in the dynamics of communities. From outside they
may appear unrealistic, but they have a compelling reality for the
individuals concerned. Their reality derives from the experience of a
world of 'objects' inside the individual. The more disturbed the
individual, the more he feels his internal world to be fragile and
threatened.

These phantasies, embedded in the personality, are responsible
for the intolerable feelings externalized in dramatizations. The

members of a community collectively express their nightmare personal worlds and their efforts to evade them.

5

Dramatization and defence mechanisms

The examples in the last chapter show how the individual finds himself assigned a role in a dramatization. His experience is further formed through positions he is required to take up in the community patterns.

This chapter will develop the psychoanalytic framework begun in the last chapter. It has become necessary to look at the interface between the community phenomena and individual experience.

The origins of the therapeutic community were in early psychoanalytic ideas (see for example, Main, 1977), but since those early days in the 1940s more recent psychoanalytic developments have passed the therapeutic community by. The approach which I am developing in this book is one which links the therapeutic community into psychoanalytic concepts again – but ones that have developed in the last half a century. In an early paper (Hinshelwood, 1972) I sketched out this psychoanalytic framework.

I will begin here with the phenomena we have been looking at in part I. This starting point concerns the psychoanalytic concept of defence mechanisms as they occur in community dynamics.

Psychological defence mechanisms

In writing about his own community, the Arbours Crisis Centre, Joe Berke says of the clients that they 'often use mechanisms of projective and introjective identification to communicate and dramatize their distress ... therapists have to become sensitive to these non-verbal channels of communication' (Berke, 1982).

He described the members as dramatizing their distress, and thus he too discriminated between enacted, non-verbal channels of communication and the verbal life of the community. These are two different levels of relating that exist alongside each other, and they correspond to the poles of the dimension discussed in chapter 2.

Projective and introjective identifications are psychological defence mechanisms lying at the core of the personality. They are the mechanisms upon which the process of dramatization rests. Psychological defence mechanisms are techniques that the human mind employs to avoid self-awareness. Projective and introjective identifications are community processes and concern the experience of personal identity. These particular defences are part and parcel of dramatization; or conversely dramatization is a manifestation of these defence mechanisms at the community level. Community and personality are linked by these processes of identification.

In this chapter I shall describe and illustrate the basic defence mechanisms operative in the human mind. They include projective and introjective identification. In addition there are two others – splitting and idealization. I shall start with splitting.

Splitting

E 5.1 Splitting off a role

At a meeting following an open day at the hospital, Rosemary, a nurse, produced a copy of the hospital magazine that had been on sale to the public. In it there had been two satirical articles, both of them making rather cruel ridicule of Rosemary – as well as others. She was indignant that such material was on sale to the public, and she was not amused. Outspoken in the hospital as an upholder of a previous order of things, she believed that the present order was misguided. She was given to state bluntly and uncompromisingly how things should be. Although well-meaning, her approach gave the impression of repressiveness. She did indeed have a degree of rigidity, and this was well known and disliked amongst the patients and staff. The staff meeting on this occasion took up her protest with wide differences of opinion over slander, censorship and editorial freedom (the editor had been a patient).

The outcome of the staff meeting was that there may or may not have been some degree of slander in the magazine and that the attention of the editor should be drawn to this possibility. Naturally this was a task that would require some flexibility and diplomatic tact, yet the meeting chose Rosemary herself to carry this delicate message to the editor. There is no doubt that given her rigidity and repressiveness, and her upset over the issue, this could only guarantee the deepening of her reputation.

At this time the staff had split between those campaigning for the new approach of the permissive therapeutic community and those adhering to the older, more rigid and paternalistic ways. This split was crystallized in the cleavage between Rosemary and the rest of the members of this staff meeting.

Split forms of caring

Once established, opinions amongst the staff became polarized into roles pressed upon separate individuals. On one side, the majority felt themselves to be in the right for being permissive and friendly to their patients, while any unpleasantness could be deflected towards Rosemary. On the other side, Rosemary felt herself to be in the right for upholding high standards, while attributing any problem to the sloppiness of her opponents.

The split had the advantage that it allowed both sides to feel perfectly justified. It was defensive on both sides, since the other was always in the wrong. The separation then became dramatized by the allotting of roles to personify the community split. As a result something happened to a genuine and judicious permissiveness. It was deprived of a firm kindness by being split into either rigidity on one side or sloppiness on the other. Neither are valuable attitudes.

Polarized roles

This particular split did not stop there. The following example concerns Rosemary, too, and is from the same week. It can be seen how, without any conscious intention, Rosemary is once more especially selected to perform a certain role in the dramatization of this split relationship.

E 5.2 **The child's contact lens**

Two days later at another staff meeting, Rosemary was reporting how she had been assisting a patient, Diana, whose three and a half year old daughter wore a contact lens that occasionally needed removing. Taking it out had been a traumatic event for all three (mother, child and nurse Rosemary). Rosemary complained to the staff meeting that this sort of trauma should not occur, for the child's sake.

There was considerable discussion at that meeting concerning various points of this story. Responsibility was shifted uneasily this way and that. Eventually a conclusion was reached. The mother should be encouraged to go back and discuss it with the prescribing ophthalmologist. It was agreed that Rosemary should no longer give the mother assistance. This would further encourage the mother to go back to the eye hospital. The question then arose of who should break this news to Diana. Because she was going to be told she could no longer pass the responsibility over to the nurses, Diana would be loaded with further maternal responsibility. She may very well feel rejected unless she was told in a very sensitive way. This was resolved, like the last example, in what seemed the worst possible way – although nobody at the time seemed to be aware of it. Rosemary was again asked to do the 'dirty work' for the staff, to tell the patient the unsatisfactory decision. It could not have been better contrived to reinforce Rosemary's reputation as rejecting, insensitive and repressive.

Once again an active situation was being dramatized in the scapegoating of Rosemary. The staff team had split. Attitudes had become highly polarized. The majority group personified in stereotyped form: 'we are the patient's friends and we do not do harsh things to them – it is the old regime which was harsh and unkind.' On the other side (represented by Rosemary) the dramatization was:

'these new ideas are soft and someone has got to face the harsh realities – someone must say what's what.'

Splitting into exaggerated positions allowed everybody to feel an unblemished purity regarding his own position – even when there were nasty things to do. The responsibility for the bad things was then always with the other side. The example clearly demonstrated the concern for off-loading responsibility somewhere else.

This was truly a psychological defence, one organized collectively by the social group for the individuals' benefits.

Projection

Splitting is commonly associated with the defence mechanism known as projection. The example here demonstrates how the processes we have been considering represent a belief in some kind of transfer of something from one group (or person) to some other group which thereby loses its own proper identity. What is transferred is important from our point of view because it is a relocated piece of personal experience. The end result is a conscious awareness that it is someone else who is experiencing it. In the example the experience transferred is the feeling of a shatteringly distressing inadequacy – just like the sort of experience referred to in chapter 1 during and after the meeting that 'went wrong' (E 1.1). This example concerns one such post-meeting staff discussion.

E 5.3 A collective projection

A half-hour staff meeting, which followed a tense community meeting, began in an unpromising way. For five minutes or so a number of separate conversations seemed to be going on simultaneously, each appearing to be animated, excited and involving. Coffee was being poured out for everyone from a table in the centre of the room and there was a good deal of moving about. The general impression of disorder and tension was intense. In the course of pouring out coffee one of the members of the team, Rose, had to go to the kitchen for some more milk. On returning she complained that the kitchen staff had been disobliging and unorganized! Sheila then recalled that it was not the only case of this happening recently. Thelma said that she knew that one of the domestic staff in the kitchen was leaving at the end of the week. By this time the character of the staff meeting had changed completely. There was a unified concentration on the topic. A concerned discussion about what was going wrong in the kitchen began in earnest. Soon there was the suggestion that the administrative officer (who was officially responsible for the kitchen staff) should be asked to come to join the meeting for the benefits of the present discussion. This was agreed quickly and decisively and one of the group was dispatched to invite him. The efficiency of the group could hardly have been greater. Possible tensions and difficulties which might have beset the kitchen staff were isolated and discussed, and sensible practical solutions were suggested. The administrative officer arrived. In fact he did make it his business to know what was bothering the kitchen staff and he was well aware of their mood. It turned out that the explanations that the staff meeting had chewed over were wholly surmise and largely incorrect. It seemed unlikely that there was anything seriously 'going wrong' in the kitchen. However, the enthusiasm of the staff meeting was unabashed and the helpful solutions continued to be put forward. Hardly anyone noticed that they were solutions to non-existent problems.

There are a number of important features to note in this example: (i) the sudden reversal from chaotic disorganized activity to coherent group discussion involving everyone; (ii) the discovery of something going wrong in another group – neither the staff meeting itself nor the preceding community meeting; (iii) the absorbed attention paid to that other group which was quite outside the responsibility of the staff meeting; and (iv) the imperviousness to reality when it was eventually presented.

The group dealt collectively with the 'bad experience' the members had just suffered in the community meeting. Their method was projection – what went wrong was another group, in fact quite incidental to the problem and elsewhere in the hospital. It was a happy chance that produced this other troubled group. Once found, the staff group exploited it very effectively for their own comfort. Having projected the trouble into the kitchen, the staff meeting did not leave it alone but identified with it, discussing it, thinking how the domestics must be feeling, what was troubling them. And this was sustained in spite of the reality.

Collective psychological defence mechanisms

The interest in the trouble in the kitchen was not intended primarily to deal with the kitchen trouble, but with the problem in the troubled staff. This was a projective identification. The staff continued to identify the troubled feelings but they no longer had to own them. Collectively they could support each other's view that the trouble was elsewhere and that the bad experience and the impulses to disorganize were located in the kitchen group. They had then defended themselves from a conscious awareness of their own experience and could work on solutions at a more comfortable emotional distance.

In each of the meetings described Rosemary was used to absorb the painful experience of being firm or harsh on behalf of the majority of the staff team. It is of some interest that Rosemary had her own way of dealing with this painful experience, with the result that she didn't have to experience consciously any pain associated with it either. She used the possibilities of the situation for a defensive re-projection of sloppy permissiveness back into the majority of the staff.

In these examples the social group had taken on psychological defence mechanisms, and the communality of defensiveness contributed to social cohesion. This idea of a social defence system was first described by Jaques (1955). Looking at it from the point of view of the members he says:

> *Individuals may put their internal conflicts into persons in the external world, unconsciously follow the course of the conflict by means of projective identification, and re-internalise the course and outcome of the externally perceived conflict by means of introjective identification.* (p. 497)

And from the point of view of the social group:

*Societies provide institutionalised roles whose occupants are
sanctioned, or required, to take into themselves the projected
objects or impulses of other members. The occupants of such roles
may absorb the objects and impulses – take them into themselves
and become either the good or bad object with corresponding
impulses.* (p. 497)

Thus, important among the characteristics of these defence mechanisms and the dramatizations they give rise to is their collective nature.
The group operates as a whole.

Introjection

There is a special gain to the individuals in submerging their own
personal defence mechanisms in the collective ones. When Jaques says
'that the gain for the individual in projecting objects and introjecting
their careers in the external world, lies in the unconscious co-operation
with other members of the institution or group who are using similar
projection mechanisms', he is speaking of introjection. The group
actually provides an internal support to the individual's own personal
defence mechanisms: 'the other members are also taken inside, and
legitimate and reinforce attacks upon internal persecutors, or support
manic idealisation of loved objects thus reinforcing denial of destructive impulses against them' (p. 497).

Dramatization and the internal world

This last passage from Jaques is complicated. He is describing a world
of drama going on inside the individual complementing the external
dramatizations I have described in the external world of the community. Jaques is using the concept of an internal world to be
described in the next chapter.

The last example illustrated this point. The individual member
came out of the distressing community meeting feeling shattered.
Each then contributed individually to a fragmentary initial discussion
which disorganized the structure around him by chatting and milling
around. He got relief from this through the appearance of the other
troubled group in the distance. Such a defence, however, was greatly

enhanced in strength and also in speed by the other members doing the same. He introjected these others at the same moment that they introjected him. Hearing confirmation from the other members, in effect the latter became agents inside him supporting his own mechanisms. This collective identifying together in which the individual accrues internal benefits from an external supporting object, is an introjective identification.

Jaques's work came from his study of a factory. Later, his co-worker Menzies (1960) studied the nursing service of a hospital, and pointed to similar collective psychological defence mechanisms. They both concluded that formally created social institutions are used by their members to establish permanent ways of working that provide for the individuals' defensive needs.

Forced introjection

Menzies also developed an understanding of introjective processes and showed how the collective defences in the nursing service were so much needed that no individual was able to stand out against them. Recruitment and training of new nurses involved unconscious induction into this defence system. Some student nurses, she pointed out, were made very uncomfortable by this pressure and dropped out of the nurse training. Menzies called this form of coercion 'forced introjection'. We have seen in the first two chapters examples of individuals becoming stuck very uncomfortably in roles in the community dramatizations.

The dramatizations I have described in therapeutic community meetings show how informal structures come to be created to provide these defences of projective and introjective identification. It was the ideas of Jaques and Menzies, both of them psychoanalysts, which became the starting point for the project undertaken here of applying psychoanalysis to the therapeutic community. We will return to these ideas when I come to speak of boundaries and barriers (see below, chapter 13).

Idealization

Thus far the mechanisms of splitting, projective identification and introjective identification have been shown to be ingredients in the defensiveness of social groups and to be implicated in dramatization. We now come to an example of the last of the important psychological defence mechanisms implicated in social defence systems and dramatizations: idealization. The following is really a detail from a later example (see E 18.1, 'Tackling the attendance problem'), used here to isolate one aspect of the community.

E 5.4 The community as paradise

Collectively there seemed to be a profound commitment to the community. People did not leave. Yet many of the members did not turn up each day. Although one might presume that the longest standing members were the most committed, in fact it was just these long-term attenders who were the most irregular. Having shown no signs of benefiting after one or two years, it might have seemed reasonable for them to take themselves off. Yet they did not go. It might have been reasonable to discuss their progress with them. However, all such moves were deeply resisted by the community, as a whole. Something irrational seemed to be going on.

Collective attitudes were involved. The outside world was such an unfriendly place one wouldn't wish one's worst enemy there, so the community mythology had it. The community itself seemed to be pictured as a Garden of Eden paradise. Such a myth was laughably out of key with reality. A particular incident showed this clearly. One member, Don, was about to be discharged in circumstances which suggested he had failed in his treatment, and which repeated his sense of failure at university and elsewhere. He objected over many days, and it came to a head with a piece of physical violence which actually did no harm to anybody, but very possibly could have done serious damage. He frightened a lot of people. Interestingly, the community meeting next day turned a blind eye to the incident and to the fear it caused. It was not mentioned. Overtly it was driven underground by patients and staff. The inclement conditions for patients in the outside world were discussed instead. The notion of a haven of friendliness and peace was particularly emphatic.

This view of paradise so moved the staff that they resolved after this particular meeting to tighten up and toughen up. Things should not be so comfortable for patients that they refuse to leave. They took some measures which in fact had no effect. The extra toughness drove the idealization of the community to further reaches, and there was even more emphasis on the benign and peaceful haven.

The cyclical aspect of the process will be formalized in chapter 11 (Fig. 11.3). Here we are concerned with how the standard view of the community was compelled collectively towards an idealization. The wish to remain oblivious to terrifying things was quite immune to the evidence of reality. As with the example of collective projection the capacity to remain in touch with reality was put out of action. This is again defensive.

The idealization rested on a projection of all nasty things into the outside world. In this myth the outside world became increasingly hostile in proportion with the violence and distress emerging inside the community.

The need to defend

To be discharged seemed like a sentence of death. The idealization allowed everyone in the community to feel identified with something so wonderfully good that each one could believe himself to embody just goodness. Such a polarization has been noted in previous examples of dramatizations, where roles were pushed into more and more extreme positions (see, for example, E 5.1 and 5.2 for this development in Rosemary's role).

All of these examples reveal the pressing need for a defence. It is a need to preserve an identity, an image of oneself that is reflected in the most positive light. Called narcissistic, this kind of anxiety is about the person's own personality. It is then covered over by these socially enhanced defence mechanisms.

The various psychological defence mechanisms can be seen to interlink. Splitting, projection, introjection, identification and idealization are primitive defence mechanisms because they relate historically to the defences employed by very young infants.

However, as we have discovered here, they are in no way confined to infant behaviour, but are very common in ordinary social processes.

Summary

This chapter has been an introduction to the way in which psychoanalytic concepts can bring coherence into the descriptions and understanding of group and community dynamics. Dramatization is the playing out of defence mechanisms that have been discovered in psychoanalysis. It is the enactment of anxieties and the defences against them. Some defence mechanisms may even seem clearer in the group setting than in the individual one. Splitting, projection, introjection, identification and idealization have all been illustrated as the collective defences which underpin dramatizations.

6

The individual in the community

Dramatizations place the individual personality in the community. They are a dual achievement, enacting both a community issue and also the individual's own internal object-relationships.

The community–individual relationship

It seems likely that an individual cannot really play much part in a (dramatizing) meeting unless he expresses something significant for the community mood. A response implies that he has formed an active relationship with the meeting and that that relationship is important at the moment.

What kind of a relationship is it? This is crucial information. We must ask: in what sort of drama is it central? If these questions are answered then both the state of the individual and the state of the community become clearer.

E 6.1 The man who thought he wanted to be himself

Frank commenced the meeting by saying that in two years he would be an alcoholic. He paused as if imparting to the meeting the ability to save him.

The meeting rose to the occasion and questioned him in an eminently psychiatric way. A number of suggestions about his psychological make-up and his family background (especially his fear of his father) had a theoretical tone, and Frank's own remarks sounded like careful hypotheses about himself rather than openings into a new experience of himself. The meeting had created a flatness typical of a psychiatric 'case conference' (this kind of meeting will be described further in E 9.1, 'Therapizing the individual').

What emerged with Frank was that his parents never let him 'be himself' and that alcoholism might be a defiance against this oppression. This may or may not have been an accurate discovery about this man's personality. There is no doubt that as a case conference this meeting had worked in an admirable way. However, it occurred to me during the meeting that there was not much benefit to Frank from this theoretical, though determined, attack on his problem. What struck me was the possibility that the relationship described between Frank and his parents was now going on between Frank and the meeting. I pointed out that the discussion had a highly theoretical character and that something was preventing Frank from 'being himself' in terms of his own feelings actually in the meeting. I pointed out, too, that if being himself meant being an alcoholic then perhaps his parents were right in preventing him from being himself in that respect.

It is possible to see that a part of Frank that was forbidden and a parental part that did the forbidding were present with us in the meeting. The latter was externalized in a role played by the rest of the meeting as a sweetly reasonable parent, understanding but so distant. The external dramatization had been scripted by the internal.

His response to my interpretation was to give some further information. He said he was to spend the next weekend at home with his parents in order to meet an alcoholic uncle of whom he was fond but whom his parents regarded with shame. There had been an incident at Frank's sister's wedding when this uncle had behaved badly and drunkenly. Mother had been very upset and father had rowed with the uncle.

As this flow of information came to an end, the meeting

seemed invited to apply its theories again, but this time after a short interaction, Frank made a show of anger. He then admitted that he was frightened to be angry, and that he feared he might be capable of murdering someone. Surprisingly in some respects, the case conference type of discussion did not close in again. In fact the discussion broadened out in a freer way. There was a more general involvement. The meeting was developing signs of moving towards the verbalizing mode and away from the dramatization. There was an emotionally freer exchange about anger from a number of people.

Frank's claim that his parents oppressed him and restricted him from being himself camouflaged a restriction on his part of his own anger and murderousness. Perhaps through drinking he could abolish 'being the angry part of himself'. His relationship with the meeting was stultifying – the emotional life was sapped out of the discussion. Through this use of the meeting Frank was able to oppress a dangerously lively part of himself. Looking at it from the other direction, the meeting as a whole went along with the camouflaging manoeuvre and it was only later that it appeared there was a general preoccupation with anger. Pointing out this relationship eventually allowed both sides of the situation to come out – both Frank's difficulty, and the 'here-and-now' mood of the community. Frank's fear and his self-restriction complemented something in the community at the time.

From the community angle, who might be murdered? And for what? For Frank, the relationship was with a restraining but perhaps rescuing figure – the father who wanted to prevent his son from becoming an alcoholic. For others, there was in fact an ambivalence about the community being restricting but rescuing. There were moves to strengthen the organization and to bring in a system of sanctions for an overt form of control of membership of the community.

The case conference type of dramatization suggested that something was being glossed over. The ambivalence included a wish to attack that rescuing father and murder him. Most members were therefore torn. They coped with it by identifying with one part – the rescuing father. But Frank took the other part, the would-be murderer who had to be restrained. The lifelessness of the case conference type of activity was not just defensive against the emotions. It hinted at the specific oppressiveness.

Frank found himself in a role in which he was the murderous part of himself, a part which then had to be stifled. Yet in being stifled he was a part of the whole dramatization of the community deprived of life.

The role he took on for the community gained him the support of the others in the collective action of the meeting. If he was murdering the life of the community meeting he was not alone. It was sanctioned by all who participated in the case conference dramatization. For the rest, this murder was now one step removed. Frank had seemed to perform it.

E 6.2 The disowned identity

This same meeting continued. A rather hypomanic patient, Gill, came in very late and drew attention to herself by her flippant and trivializing remarks. A staff member, Tessa, mentioned that Frank's 'paranoia' at the beginning of the meeting had changed into the fear of one's own anger. Gill remarked immediately that she had just been talking to a seriously paranoid man in the kitchen downstairs. She would go and bring him to the meeting. He needed compassion and she did not patronize him, she said. Tessa then said he must represent some part of Gill herself, and could she not talk about herself. Gill said, no, she would fetch him. But she was told she could not as the man downstairs was not part of the day community. Tessa invited Gill to talk about the man so that we could, through him, understand a little about herself. In fact, Gill was able to say very little, and soon left the meeting.

The meeting had clearly continued in the same sort of vein as earlier. Although Gill had not been in the first part of the meeting, she took on the dramatized role of 'not being some part of herself' – a part that seemed to have been left in the kitchen. This was a 'paranoid' part of her that needed compassion without being patronized. The response reveals a clash over whether Gill could be allowed to revert to the dramatizing mode. Since the meeting had moved and was now firmly anchored in the verbal, it seemed that Gill could no longer really be in the meeting at all.

Being excluded and being included

Objections are sometimes heard that a person's individuality is overlooked. He may fear being submerged in the identical mass of membership. At times it is a cry on behalf of the narcissistic elements who refuse to recognize something bigger, more powerful, wiser than they are themselves. At times, however, the complaint arises from the actual pressure put on individuals to get into roles the community meeting assigns. Their individuality in the meeting is restricted to one part of their personality (Hinshelwood, 1982).

We have seen features of the community as a whole – (i) the undifferentiated community meeting that goes wrong; (ii) latent and overt forms of hostility; (iii) dramatizations; (iv) individuals as personalized elements caught in the community drama; and (v) the rich resources available for enacting the dramatizations.

We have seen in example E 3.1 ('The suffering community') that different people were exploited on different days to express different community moods. On the second day Harriet expressed disgruntlement and indignation, and this was in contrast to the day before when Chris and Eve embodied the despair about madness and its effects. It seems that the individual comes forward who is most suited to express in this dramatizing mode something of the detailed unconscious content of the meeting.

Attending to the mood of the meeting based on the contributions of one individual does not exactly neglect that individual. Something individual about him represents the rest of the membership – yet it may be only part of him. Neither does attending to an individual really neglect the meeting – yet it studies only half a relationship that all are exploiting.

A great deal of the experience of community meetings is concerned with being out of the meeting or being in it (see E 9.4, 'Accommodating patients', and E 14.4, 'The in-group and the out-group'). These are important issues for the individual trying to find his feet in the community and the community meeting under the onslaught of all his own difficulties.

In discussing the experience of being a member of a large study group, Turquet writes:

> *At the beginning of a session, the member of a large group ... perceives himself as surrounded, therefore bounded by his own silence. While remaining within his own island of silence he is a singleton. The temptation to remain there is great, since omnipotent mastery seems still within his grasp. To step off into relatedness to others may be worth attempting, but the move carries risk. The content of this risk is not only to step from the singleton state into the yet unknown I-state [i.e. an individual in relation to others], but because the unknown has an unencompassable vastness, there is the further risk of an endless disappearance.* (1975, p. 119)

Turquet goes on to describe how the member can master the problems of boundlessness by establishing responses from others which serve to confirm his own presence and identity. Yet the risk is to be sucked into strange identities when 'group membership predominates over individual self-definition' (p. 95). In his own terms he describes the risk of being employed for group purposes in roles used for dramatizations.

There are characteristic types of role that individuals find themselves sucked into. In this chapter I shall discuss 'the monologuist' and 'the silent member'; and in the next chapter I shall discuss three other types of leadership.

The monologuist

A frequent occurrence in the free-floating kind of community meeting is the apparently interminable monologue. This appears to offer no relationship at all between the meeting and the individual. However, by looking at this in another way it can be seen to be a dramatization of a relationship excluding all other people.

E 6.3 The monologuist

In a mid-week meeting one of the more dominant patients,

Freda, came into the room with two walking sticks and her leg in plaster. She sat down and asked another patient to put a chair under her leg. She thus became very prominent and her monologue was the single focus of attention of the group for the first half an hour or so. Such a monologue had been a feature of community meetings for a little while and Freda in particular often took the role. It had become generally felt by the staff that a meeting taken up by a monologue was not valuable. However, what could be done about it?

After some twenty minutes or so, the monologue was interrupted by Tim who remarked on the manner of presentation adopted by Freda, rather than on the content of what she said. It is necessary to convey a brief impression of Freda. Her admission to the community followed her separation from a much-loved lesbian partner with whom she had lived for some thirty years. Her behaviour in the hospital had been violent and provocative of violence, which seemed both gratifying in a sado-masochistic way and also abreactive of her experience of having been abused. Her disinhibited behaviour was regularly assisted by heavy drinking before meetings. At the meeting I am reporting, Tim had been struck by a lessening of Freda's violence and provocativeness. He guessed that she had not been drinking. His impression was that she was easier to empathize with because she was not drunk. Tim confided this impression to Freda in the meeting. In her masochistic way, Freda insisted that this was a moral condemnation of her drinking. Tim protested that, if anything, he had been trying to convey a note of approval. But the condemnation issue was taken up by two or three others – who happened to be heavy drinkers. Clearly a quite delusional state of affairs was arising. Although one could say there had been a slight movement away from the monologue pattern, it had taken the direction of the familiar persecuting court-room scenario, with an accused, an accuser and an unfriendly atmosphere. The meeting could hardly be said to have changed for the better.

Later on another member of staff, Vic, made an intervention that seemed to have more success – with the result that more people joined in and verbalized something that hitherto had remained obscure within the dramatization.

Vic had thought Tim's original remark had seemed accurate

though unsuccessful, and he took it up. He remarked that, although Freda was easier to emphathize with and that most other people must have had similar experiences to suffer in their lives, in fact nobody actually responded to what Freda had been saying, or shared their own experiences of separation with Freda. After this a couple of patients agreed that they had had similar painful separations. This led into attacks on certain members of the nursing staff who were thought to lack understanding; and then to criticism of the staff in general over recent changes in the timetable which had led to confusions; and then to a brief reminiscence about a popular occupational therapist who had left the hospital the previous week.

There is an intriguing link in this illustration between the monologue pattern and the feelings of separation. The more successful interpretation was not about Freda's mental state, but about her manifest isolation within the meeting as a whole. The subsequent discussion dwelt on feelings of isolation in general and those experienced by many people specifically within the community.

Eventually a lack of contact with the staff was directly expressed. Until that point the problem must have been the belief that there was nobody there to understand it. That is a particularly poignant despair – when a belief exists that there is nobody there to understand the sense of there being nobody there. The loss of a popular member of staff and the approaching summer holiday period when a number of staff would be away reflected the internal state of loneliness and loss, and the crushing responsibility discussed in chapter 4.

Freda came to the fore as particularly suited to lead an external dramatization of this internal problem, currently stimulated in the community as a kind of whistling in the dark. This meeting does not only provide a picture of a forlorn individual dominating others with her misery. It is also a picture of a community which for the time being is not felt to provide an adequate and supportive companionship. A reverberation between internal and external seemed to have driven the whole community into this extreme state of hopeless communication, in which even the broken leg symbolized the loss of support.

The disappearance of any other identifiable companions is expressed as a dramatic fact in the silence of the monologuist's audience. They appear as cabbages, with advanced signs of disinterest, staring at the ceiling, the floor or out of the window. One could say their minds are elsewhere. And Turquet's description of the singleton remaining safely wrapped in his own silence is very apt.

For the monologuist herself, she could perhaps overcome the isolation in a boundless state of feeling that she is the meeting. There is not then a separation – instead an intoxicating swelling out as if to encompass everything, to command and control all the people and the furniture. All are furniture.

The silent member

In contrast to the monologuist is the silent member. He apparently listens endlessly, although it is probably not listening in the ordinary sense. Just like the monologuist who becomes identified with the meeting itself, the silent member is protecting a similar feeling of omnipotent mastery, as Turquet pointed out.

E 6.4 **The silent member**

Fred was a man in his thirties who remained in a withdrawn and inactive state following a psychotic episode provoked by LSD. He had been attending the hospital daily for some two years, interrupted just about a year before when he threatened his wife with an axe. He was then sent to a mental hospital for 28 days. On his return he resumed his inactivity. He whiled away community meetings, either reading a book or sleeping. On this occasion, however, the meeting was occupied by the love affair between two other patients. Gwen had just quarrelled with Harry, her lover, who had stormed out of the hospital in a rage. Gwen tremulously filled the meeting with the anxiety that he would return to the flat that night and attack her or do some other violent damage.

At the point at which the meeting was considering Gwen's role in provoking threats of violence, Fred opened his mouth for the first time in two years and said that Harry wanted to be violent. He repeated this a few moments later. It apparently added little to the way the discussion was going and was not taken up at all.

Like the silent member in example E 3.1 ('The suffering community') Fred was identified momentarily with the community when something most resembled a part of himself – the part that was violent towards his wife. In his preoccupied and distant comment, and with a flat, toneless voice he seemed to find himself easily flowing into what was going on. It was not exactly that he was only in the meeting when it touched on his problem. He did not suddenly perk up with interest at this subject from a prolonged boredom with everything else. It appeared rather that he was in a very different state of being in which he merged momentarily with the rest of the members united in concentration on this issue. At this moment he had solved the problem Turquet defined of the unintegrated member having to risk plunging into the group to find his identity. Instead Fred waited until the group came to his own identity, as it were, whereupon he could then feel merged with it.

States of merger

Communities are flooded by despair and by the exaggerated hopes of the high proportion of members who have a lot at stake. On occasions many of them cope with the urgency by merging in a way that encompasses them in an identification with the whole group at once. They may appear silent but the activity of the meeting is felt to be their own activity inside them.

The silent member retreats from the meeting to locate his mind elsewhere. He is occupied in a different way from that required by the meeting. In order to cope with feeling separated and excluded he lives in a kind of delusion that there really is no difference between himself and the rest of the meeting. The boundary has dissolved for him. When something happens in the meeting he is there only if 'it is me that is happening'. This move omnipotently evades his fear of exclusion and separation and of the loss of cohesion of the parts of himself or of the community.

Both the silent member and the monologuist break down the boundary between themselves and the meeting very extensively. Anxiety over separation mounts if there is also a fear that the community is breaking up. The lonely fragments of the community deny the anxiety in an effort to cope with it. And they do so by welding themselves into a delusional merger. All boundaries are then threatened with being dissolved into a boundless undifferentiated community. These kinds of phenomena at a community level will be discussed later (for example, in E 14.7, 'The special group of students', there is a moment of clinging against the threatened fragmentation).

At this point it is worth noting again the related experience of Eve, whose behaviour was described in example E 3.1 ('The suffering community'). She indulged in an activity in which she attempted to encompass all the others in the room, who were symbolized by all the parts of her identity encompassed in her handbag.

In dramatizations of the monologue/silence type, people are embedded in remote, unrealistic states in the community. The bizarre identification with the community means that the effectiveness, integrity and identity of the individual is even more closely linked with the effectiveness, integrity and identity of the community.

The problem of the individual in the community can now be seen in a new light. It is the problem of securing the very basis of a sense of personal identity. The problem for all individuals is to dare to distinguish themselves from the rest of the meeting. That is to say, they have to establish clearly the boundary between what they consider is internal and what external. Members are constantly struggling with one or other of two phantasies, either that the meeting is being incorporated into the individual – i.e. the external is obliterated; or that the individual is suffused throughout the meeting – i.e. he loses the sense of an internal world.

Although these are probably general experiences, they are more dominant and influential in those taking up the monologuist role or the silent member role. In the next chapter we will return to individuals who operate in a less disturbed way but who by the force of their own personalities can lead the dramatizations of the whole community into more differentiated dramatizations (as did Ellen and Esther in E 4.1 and E 4.2).

Summary

A complex relationship has begun to emerge between the individual and the community. The illustrations of the externalizations of the individuals' own internal object-relationships as dramatizations in the community as a whole may look like one-way traffic. In fact individuals are engaged in dramatized roles when they have some specific adaptability or 'valency' for the role needed by the community. That is to say, there is some happy fit between the individual's own internal phantasy relationship and the relationship needed by the community dramatization. The individual becomes something of a leader in the community for that moment. Particularly obscure is the leadership offered by the monologuist, which appears to abolish the community altogether. The silent member, too, is an obscure figure, and seems to correspond closely to the monologuist in terms of a bizarre merged relationship with the community.

7

The regime and the individual

To continue the theme of the individual–community reverberation between internal and external worlds, I shall briefly describe further types of individual identification with the group.

The individuals in the roles discussed below have a much surer judgement of the reality of life in groups than the monologuist and the silent member. With a greater capacity for working in the interpersonal area, they can have a powerful effect on the community organization – on its regime. They are able to bring the 'community personality' into line with the characteristic internal relationships of their own personalities. I picked out these types because they seem to represent 'pure cultures'.

We have seen how harsh internal criticism becomes external criticism (E 4.1, 'The persecuted victim'). The whole style of the community organization comes to be modelled upon the individual's personality. I shall be describing: (i) the leader of a very fragmented community, someone who is preoccupied with her own internal fragmentation as described by Klein (see above, p.62); (ii) a dependent and intimidating 'mafia' who promote a community for their own purposes; (iii) the rigid leader forming a focus for rigid community bureaucracy; and (iv) a community regime under the control of delinquents.

Reverberation

Reverberation between the individual and the community is not to be taken simply as a one-way process, with one individual holding the community in thrall to his internal world. That is only the surface appearance, although it is an easy mistake to make. The chosen individual and the community culture form a 'neurotic marriage'. How does this happen?

Some kind of rolling process gathers momentum, moulding the culture and the role to fit together in some final stable endpoint. A community faced with an issue such as the loss presented in E 3.1 ('The suffering community') throws up an individual to fulfil its demands. In that example several appeared in succession over the course of a few days, and were then superseded as the significance of the issue changed.

In other instances a stable state evolves. Individuals are the resources for the dramatizations. They come to be selected because they have the characteristics to fulfil the specific dramas. The leader pushed to the fore then seems to establish a command over the issues so that he can gather them in under his own personal approach. If he and the community 'fit', then it becomes a self-perpetuating process. The community's needs fit the individual's needs, and the cycle proceeds in a runaway fashion. It is driven by two mechanisms: the selection of the personality by the process, and channelling of the process by the personality. With the right personality linked into the right process, the system runs to one of a limited number of endpoints (discussed below, see chapter 19).

The dramatizations the individual offers have unconscious defensive advantages. The cost to the community members is being forced to adopt this leader's style of defensiveness. Often this aggravates the initial problem.

The community will accept a leadership of this kind when the community issue shows a close correspondence with the leader's own problem so that he has, as it were, special practice at it. For example, the threats of community disorganization put Gwynneth, the schizoid ruler in the next example, in a special position because of her own fears about personally fragmenting.

A probable further condition enhancing the 'fit' between community and individual is that a major proportion of individuals have similar personalities and therefore the internal relationships and defences have a high degree of conformity throughout the members. (Witness the rather rigid states of the community led by the bureaucratic constitutionalist mentioned later in this chapter, and the phenomena described in chapter 16).

De Jong (1983) has described an interesting community problem in which the membership accumulated an increasing proportion of people with eating problems. It was not clear to the staff until some time later that this selective bias had resulted in the development of radical changes around meal times and attitudes to eating in the community culture. The seduction of the staff who were caught up in the process without realizing it was impressive from our point of view. The accumulation of a large proportion of people with a similar introjective problem interestingly led to a culture which idealized its abilities while remaining unable to take in the features of reality.

It is likely that the remarkable consistency that is found between the Synanon* type of drug-treatment houses, results as much from the selective consistency as from the vigorous culture of conformism.

The cruel twist for the patient in trouble is that he comes to a community which, in spite of himself, he twists into a distorted version of what it should be. This may not only come from his misperceptions; through these misperceptions he may actually contribute to the development of a pathological organization. As Oscar Wilde grimly noted, 'everyone kills the one he loves'. The member of the community makes of his one hope a replica of his own internal tragedy.

Group chaos

The first type of special culture leader I call the schizoid ruler. He presides over constant group chaos.

---

*The Synanon type of therapeutic community was evolved in America in the 1960s to deal with drug abusers and alcoholics. The selection was therefore for a very homogeneous group of people dependent on pharmacological substances. These communities evolved a very rigid, hierarchical and quite punitive regime, which gave rise to remarkably consistent offshoots across the world thriving in all sorts of national cultures (see Sugarman, 1974; Glaser, 1977; Hinshelwood, 1986).

E 7.1 **The schizoid ruler**

Gwynneth was a very disturbed girl in her early twenties whose life, thoughts and conversation were in permanent disarray. She controlled a matching community around her. Meetings were particularly frustrating and notable for the high levels of tension, the lack of co-ordination or theme, the interruptions, the multiple conversations, the frequent calls for strong leadership and the total lack of loyalty to anyone who made an attempt to lead and organize.

Staff meetings were infected in spite of their professional structure. The community organization itself suffered, through hindrance of the opportunities to organize and through an intimidating scorn for anyone who showed an allegiance to the community system. Anybody trying to organize, staff or patient, found himself cut off and isolated in ridicule. All this seemed to be orchestrated by Gwynneth, whose ability to rule the community in this way contrasted with her inability to rule anything constructively. She had an immense personal charm, a vivid attractiveness and a strident provincial accent. Her capacity to use these dominating gifts to trounce constructive efforts was matched only by her despair at finding herself left in the midst of a chaos no-one could clear up.

Gwynneth's intense feelings always aroused deep concern in the community, and carried with them the anxiety that there was no-one around to help her tolerate them or abate their intensity. She gave the impression of living in a desolate or ruined place, and she seemed to experience the fear that she had already overwhelmed the rescuers she depended on. Her only defence seemed to be withering contempt for the community and its organization and for anyone she might need to turn to. This contempt did indeed seem to emphasize the overwhelming quality of her character. She would eventually lapse from contempt into an exhausted, empty futility.

In the context of the community at this time she was highly influential, dominating it with the quality of her anxieties and then with her contempt. She advocated an extreme permissiveness and at the same time (or in rapid alternation) she experienced an intense languid despair at the feeble achievements of her permissive regime.

Any aspects of organization which put constraints on individuals were strenuously opposed. The efforts of the committee to organize simple systems for getting the washing up done, for example, were denigrated, and over a period of time became half-hearted and ineffective. In particular, any effort by the staff to defend the timetable and keep the programme in order were derided, and the derision was only interrupted by complaints about boredom and the lack of organized facilities.

The hindrance to anything emerging from the melting pot came from panic at the uncertainty that change, rival ideas and experimentation bring. Gwynneth's personality aptly represented these anxieties and at the same time allowed her to create a community in her own image. Her despair at handling her own internal state could be expressed through the medium of despair at the community's fragmentation.*

Gwynneth, the individual, was not the simple cause of this. When conditions in the community altered it became quite possible to bring the system firmly under control and contain this individual as just another patient once again. The community itself had been going through its own battles over authority, structure and organization. The forthcoming appointment of a new consultant to take charge of the day service posed a challenge for the staff in post. The staff had been existing in a 'leaderless' interregnum for some time. During this period Gwynneth therefore performed an act 'fit' for the community. In her own internal world all her capacities to link together, to get things to work, to form coherent organized thought, were attacked from within. In Guntrip's account (1961) the characteristic object-relationship of this kind of personality is 'a struggle to preserve an ego' (see also Klein, 1946).

---

*Aspects of this example will be considered further in the section on 'Fragility and fragmentation' in chapter 15, p.189.

The psychopathic mafiosi

Later examples (for instance, see E 20.1, 'Therapy is a community process') illustrate the way in which some individuals appear to take hold of the community in a callous way and, without thought for others, to turn the organization to their own personal advantage. This leader gets himself quite special concessions: for lateness, absences, for transgressions of drinking rules, for getting unwarranted accommodation in the in-patient unit. No doubt they may supply themselves with money or drugs through exploiting and intimidating other patients. In this case the regime of the community is of a particular and matching kind. It appears to be apathetic and lacking a sense of serious purpose. The organization flags for want of renewal (not through attacks and ridicule as in the last example). Allegiance is to the slogan: everyone for himself, with the justification that the individual's wants are paramount and should be protected from frustration – 'after all the place is to help people, surely not to punish or to control them'. Such plaintive slogans are wielded callously like sledge-hammers by a privileged gang leader or by a small gang establishing its hegemony. No-one must enquire further than the interests of the person who can make the loudest noises. The majority of people go to the wall and to all intents and purposes give up. This process can also be seen in E 11.1, 'The hamstrung community'.

E 7.2 The ruling mafiosi

At one point the community was going through a phase in which the system and the discipline was loosening up. This eventually reached alarming proportions. The institutions which maintained the community needed support. The problem that arose, however, was a serious lack of involvement on a community scale.

Some of the more dependable members of the community had recently left. The community meetings were taken over by a small number of people – perhaps almost a parody of the leadership that had just left. Most of the other members remained silent.

The three people who did come to the fore began to dominate the meetings by letting forth in one way or another about the difficulties which they personally experiencea in being part of this community. Their pleas rested on their own special symptoms and they seemed to canvass for change that would entirely suit themselves. With little obviously in common, they nevertheless appeared to operate an intuitive collaboration. One of the three was a very dependent, imploring, neurotic girl, one a man with mild brain-damage who was terrified by his own violent outbursts, and the third was a cold-blooded threatening psychopath. As a selection from which to choose leadership for the community they did not amount to much, and one would imagine that they could easily have been dispatched from the centre of the stage. However they were not. Indeed the reverse, the community acted up to the dramatization.

What kept the community inactive and ineffective was that these three represented something for the community. Their leadership amounted to a plea that their own personal discomforts be the prime responsibility of the community, and this was allowed to happen, or rather it was dramatized. In the community drama they represented a triumphant and perverse dominance of psychological disturbance and infantile self-indulgence over sensible organization. This is a delusional view which gives priority of place to mental disorder, and it is akin to the myth of the community as paradise (E 5.4). Instead of sticking to the task of treating mental disorders, the task of gratifying them was substituted.

Here is another case of the familiar matching of individual personalities to the roles in a dramatized community dynamic. The individuals concerned had in them characteristic internal object-relations which could be externalized into the community regime to express a need of the community at this time. Their internal world functioning in a corresponding way could be externalized directly into the community regime. The internal world of the psychopathic leader is specifically one of domination by very destructive aspects of his personality, which, as it were, intimidate his own more constructive aspects. It seems that such people try

to get rid of their concern and love for their objects by killing their loving dependent self and identifying themselves almost entirely with the destructive narcissistic part of the self which

provides them with a sense of superiority and self-admiration ...
The destructive narcissism of these patients appears often highly
organized, as if one were dealing with a powerful gang
dominated by a leader, who controls all the members of the gang
to see that they support one another in making the criminal
destructive work more effective and powerful... The main aim
seems to be to prevent the weakening of the organization and to
control the members of the gang so that they will not desert the
destructive organization and join the positive parts of the self or
betray the secrets of the gang.   (Rosenfeld, 1971, p. 174)

In struggling to describe the internal world of certain patients this psychoanalyst working with patients individually has resorted to a group analogy. The internal world is thus so immediately a source of the external regime.

The psychopathic leader of the kind just described does not always get his or her own way. The community may be provoked in a different direction, and a different regime results (see the final example E 20.1, 'Therapy is a community process', which demonstrates a community attempting to deal with such a person). In this case the community protects itself against the simple enactment of the leader's delinquent object-relations by becoming rigidly unaccommodating. The iron fist of the community can come down on these personality types and control their excesses (see 'The iron fist', chapter 16, p. 200).

The rigidity of the community regime constructed by those with this kind of personality is highlighted when they are concentrated in a therapeutic community. And the therapeutic community has, to some extent, created its reputation with psychopaths. But there are other kinds of personalities that, gathered in some concentration, will externalize a different regime, which shows a rigidity of a different kind. These are the more obsessional types of personality.

The bureaucratic constitutionalist

On the surface, the role I shall call 'the bureaucratic constitutionalist' appears less pernicious in its effect on the community. Now and then there arise calls to legislate and issue proclamations, to construct a constitution, or rigidly to write every patient a contract to be signed and enforced detailing what he is expected to do in the next week/month/phase of his treatment. These leaders are often the bearers of a flame of initiative and reason. Such proposals are not to be written off immediately, for they may develop into fertile practices. However, they may also cause enormous and protracted problems (see, for example, E 16.1, 'The bureaucratic constitution').

The individuals behind these moves are not so prominent as the previous types – they exemplify the faceless bureaucrat. Yet they are clearly identifiable within the community and become the reference point for all the problems that crop up. They do not get into trouble in the community in the same way as the others, for their own way of acting out is especially orderly, thoughtful, punctual and supportive of the staff. These characteristics are nothing but laudable, except ... The problem is one of defining the problem in this orderliness.

What this leader does for the community is to take any problem and convert it into an organizational procedure. It effectively quashes and smoothes over the anxieties that might otherwise be properly held up for examination. These leaders carefully place themselves sympathetically just outside the emotional range of what is going on. They are thus perfectly poised to pick it up at the right moment and convert it into a new regulation or a contract. However inventive or creative this may be, it is also evasive and particularly dodges potential self-confrontation. Equally, the perpetrators hinder others' treatment by offering structural changes in the organization when personal crises loom ahead. They might be said to hinder the community activity by smothering it with a lofty concern. For concern is one thing they do not lack. In the reign of terror example (see E 10.1) the aim was to dispose of the discomfort everyone felt. It happened in that instance to entail prematurely terminating many people's chance of treatment! But, no matter – the intention was to ease distress, by not facing it.

Once more, this leader comes forward to lead a regime at the right time. As a result, the community's task is perverted; it is made to withdraw from exploring the emotional world within and between people; instead it is diverted towards adapting and creating community procedures.

Summary

I have discussed how an individual may come to dominate, with his or her own characteristic internal object-relationship, not only the community meeting but indeed the whole organization. It is in this sense that he can be said to create his own regime. Particular kinds of individual were described – schizoid, psychopath, demanding dependant and obsessional bureaucrat – whose regimes are dominated on a less individual basis than it might appear.

I suggest that the leader remains dependent on the community issues that he is peculiarly adept at evading. A cyclical activity probably takes place: the community issue is relieved by the typical evasive manoeuvring of one individual who guides it into an expression of his own internal world through the community dramatization; frequently this enhances the community problem giving rise to even more exacting evasive manoeuvres.

PART III

Despair, idealization and morale

8

Staff as the transference object

The particular reasons why a new patient joins a therapeutic community give him cause for special expectations. These bring out in high relief some very important features of community culture. The new patient arrives in the community having had it forced upon him that in his own achievements and in his own life he is at the end of the line. However hard he tried in the past to make something of his mortal time, it is now in ruins. He will be tortured by the despair of this. He will desperately clutch at any illusive straw.

His conscious appreciation of the situation is remote and clouded. He will perceive only the tip of the iceberg. At the core of his difficulties is often a belief that he has lost or is about to lose the really good thing in his life (see chapter 4). The one really good and comforting thing which makes him feel warm and wanted inside is felt to be missing. Coloured by this initial experience, he feels there is no good thing or person to turn to. He looks for some understanding external 'object' to help with and relieve the experience. In his heart of hearts, however, he invariably doubts the existence of an 'object' or person who can understand him – that is, no-one who can understand that he feels there is no-one to help him. When hopelessness spirals in on itself like this, it becomes necessary to find some quite superhuman figure who can break through it all. This is the expectation that a new patient will bring with him when he enters the door of his therapeutic community, and was discussed above in chapter 4.

The member of staff is confronted by the patient's expectations, and finds that they are placed upon the staff member himself. In this chapter I want to explore this position that the staff member finds himself in. As part of the staff team he is ensnared in a particularly engaging dramatization made out of the structure of the community. The division between staff and patients, just by being there, attracts the 'splitting' which is the foundation of the roles used in dramatizations. The division in the community becomes a hook to hang roles and dramatizations upon. In this way, the staff team comes to be used in just the way the psychotherapist in any other form of psychotherapy is used. It is a case of transference – and the staff team or individual staff members become transference objects. Because the staff have a particularly explicit responsibility for the functioning and effectiveness of the community, they are invariably identified as the superhuman omnipotent saviour that the patient invariably seeks.

As therapists in the various psychotherapeutic and sociotherapeutic fields of learning, they have their professional roles. Realistically, as members of staff they have a joint responsibility to attend to the organization and to see that it is discussed and serviced as needed. They have both professional and service roles – and for the purpose of the latter they will be assigned organizational roles, deriving their responsibilities from the structure of authority in the community.

It is most important to get these organizational and therapeutic roles clear, because only then can the members of staff begin to disentangle themselves from the tentacles of the patients' vast expectations of them. Such expectations come out in the various community dramatizations.

As the group within the community with a particular concern for the organization, the staff may very well be regarded as coupled (like parents perhaps) in a staff-community marriage – as a father who is protective of mother, or as a mother who is nourishing and caring for father or for another sibling. Many such 'family' phantasies are encountered in the community. However, this is not the only level of phantasy. There are primitive levels of anxiety (arising from the paranoid-schizoid or depressive object-relations discussed in chapter 4) at which the community is experienced as the one really good thing to which the patient can cling in his efforts to cope with his own noxious mental experiences. Depending on the shared beliefs active at any particular time, the staff may be seen as crucial to the ability of the community to act as this relieving container – or to its failure to function in this way. There arises extreme interest in and involved observation of and phantasizing about the efforts of staff, their personalities, their organization and their interrelationships.

The fragile transference object

The members' concern for the community is closely bound up with concern for the staff group as an effective team which will promote and protect an effective community on which the patients can depend. Members have invested large amounts of time in the community, large chunks of their lives and youth, maybe six months or a year. Such an investment is a considerable one. What can really be expected in return? I have often been impressed by the apparent lack of awareness, or at least, discussion of this by the staff. No doubt this omission is to do with the sense of responsibility and the feeling that they, the staff, must come up with the goods in equal proportion to the faith manifested by the hopeful patient. It is then difficult for the staff to empathize easily with patients who at some point reach a crisis of doubt about the community. The difficulty the staff have in sharing in these doubts with patients often leads to a chronic disjunction or mutual incomprehension between staff and patients. It only leads patients to doubt further whether the staff can understand them. Often staff do have doubts themselves, but feel they shouldn't let the patients know this – once again leaving patients high and dry with their own uncomprehended doubts. The patient may feel that the staff cannot bear to be doubted. It may be true that it is very painful for the staff, especially since it touches on their own unrealistic demands on themselves to be omnipotent.

It is in fact quite a common feature of therapeutic communities that patients feel themselves to be in relation to a fragile staff group which can bear no criticism or questioning about the community that they hold so dear and feel so responsible for. Frequently the patients feel, in secret, that they must support the staff (which perhaps they do) and yet feel the staff do not want the patients to know of their need.

The staff group, as the transference object, allows such phantasies to be elaborated and woven into very complex unspoken attitudes

– which only come through in the dramatized form. Unverbalized, these phantasies can accumulate to massive and then terrifying proportions. The more they go unspoken, the more they are felt to be unspeakable.

If staff are energetic in sharing decision-making and passing responsibility over to the consensus, it may at times be felt as if the staff group have thrown in the sponge. They may be felt to be overwhelmed by their task and their responsibilities, or to have suffered more than they can bear of aggressive and uncooperative patients. After all as we have seen, patients do believe in their heart of hearts that they contain something overwhelming.

At times, the staff as a group may seem extremely exclusive, allowing no involvement in the important areas of discussion (anxious staff do sometimes hog the discussion time). Patients may feel that they are not trusted, that the staff feel them to be a liability.

The working relationships and the style of teamwork in the staff group is of crucial significance to the patients, and they keep a close eye on everything, interpreting the staff according to the community mood of the moment. Disagreements, indecisiveness, rivalries, love affairs, schisms, reconciliations, as well as comparisons of professional competence, are all enormously important to members. They scrutinize with endless care and speculation. The hopes of the patients, especially at first, rest with exaggerated weight on the current state and competence of the staff, individually and as a team.

However, staff members, out of genuine or false modesty, wish to minimize the embarrassing importance attributed to them. Yet they cannot do so without a dismissal which is itself significant for the patients. The patients believe that their interest in the staff is unwanted or is intrusive upon the staff's privacy. The problem is then only driven further underground, and the staff seem even more sensitive.

The staff need to overcome their modesty, but further, they need the strength to face the scrutiny to which they are subject, warts and all. Their problem lies in feeling guilt and responsibility for their patients. They fear being found out to be only ordinarily human – rather than omnipotently superhuman.

Often staff dodge this kind of discussion, using various means open to them. They may make a studied recourse to the individual patient and his symptoms and failures. Although this may be perfectly valid, actually in the context it can feel to the patient like a deliberate distraction on the part of the staff member, who is then believed to be using the patient for his own comfort. Patients actually need the experience of someone less defensive who can face the possibility, at least, of being ordinary and fallible. At other times staff may engage in a flight into overconfidence, simply denying their struggles with their own experience. They recall successful times from the past. Or they may wheel in an external third party (there is always one handy somewhere) who is awkwardly hindering or threatening the community. Alternatively, the staff may split, so that it is the 'other staff members' who are having their own problems. Sometimes this is expressed by joining in a collective bemoaning of the community, or of the staff, or the numbers of suicides, or the numbers of drop-outs or failures – a device which is a hidden way of getting at someone in authority who has responsibility for all this, and who, by implication is therefore not doing his job well enough.

Supporting the staff

It is understandable for patients to fear that as partners in the work they must have troubled and demoralized the staff. If they feel that they have interfered with the staff they feel responsible for their malaise and fragility. In addition they may greatly, and in secret, despair over being able to restore the staff group on whom their own security and hopes seem to depend so heavily. These kinds of phantasies may lead the patients to reject the staff altogether, or to bicker and blame each other in indirect ways, or to take up any of the other manifestations of demoralization which appear when belief in the community sags and a vital element is felt to be out of order.

Staff confidence

It needs to be said that there is some truth in the view that the staff's difficulties in their work derive from the problems of or interference from the patients. After all, by the time someone ends up in a psychiatric unit of any kind they are people who have defeated the hope and optimism of the rest of society – and of a series of helpers before they get to a therapeutic community. They must, therefore, be a threat to the confidence of the community and be likely to test the efforts of all their helpers there too.

Perhaps one of the most difficult aspects of being a patient is finding the hopes and the confidence of the staff resting on one's shoulders. This does happen. There is no reason why it should not. For example, a community meeting is a difficult situation – for anyone, the staff members included. The most urgent problem for the member of staff is to ensure that he exists in some recognizable role. His value as a therapist, psychiatrist, nurse, or whatever may be very vulnerable to the exposure he feels he undergoes in the public situation. To get no response to his contributions can be very unnerving. He can feel as much at sea as the newest and most confused patient. The staff member's own feelings about himself in his job rest heavily and repeatedly on the way the community handles him.

It is often dutifully accepted that what a staff member says in the community meeting is more weighty than other contributions. Reactions may perhaps be graded according to some supposed heirarchy amongst the staff. The staff also have the good fortune of a ready-made lobby. They work as a team, often with prior discussions to resort to. This psychological cohesiveness of the staff team supports the confidence of each member. When the staff group begins to fail in its function, some staff members may find themselves in difficulties in the community meeting. Their hesitation and uncertainty may well become noticeable, especially to patients who have invested a particular confidence in that member of staff.

In a therapeutic community which runs small group therapy, the small groups may go up in the valuation of what the community provides, and other events may decline (see Manning, 1976). At these times the valuation of small group leaders also goes decidedly up. Inevitably, for their own reasons, the small group leaders enhance their own security through this trend, and everyone wants to be one. The staff group effectively divides in two – the high status small group leaders, and the rest with lower status. From the point of view of the patient accepting the prevailing community values, it is important to him that his small group leader should appear competent when encountered in comparison with other staff in the context of the whole community. A collusive system may develop across the whole community to establish the value of the small group leaders. A 'gentleman's code' may be established in which no-one shall say anything defamatory or undermining about someone else's group leader.

E 8.1 The gentleman's code

At one point one of the small group leaders who was not in fact popular within the community system of values decided to give up running a small group. It was only as a result of this that there developed a freedom in the community to express reservations about this member of staff which had been harboured for a long period of time. In the next few months he was carefully edged to the periphery of the meetings.

The structured transference object

Although comparisons between members of staff provide one of the major preoccupations and anxieties in the community – perhaps for members of staff as well – they are virtually never expressed openly, either in the community meeting or in the staff meeting. The curtain drawn across the topic enables a further kind of activity to develop. Because dissension and rivalry between members of staff is covert, a member of staff can appeal indirectly to the community for personal support in order to acquire advantage in relation to another member of the staff. Specific topics or clinical judgements about individual patients become arenas for this covert contest. Even when it is very obvious to all involved, it is seldom mentioned directly in a way that could contribute to a resolution. The outcome of this kind of situation is one of two conditions. On the one hand, the contest splits the community in its allegiance to different members of staff, which cannot be discussed, and a community results which becomes living evidence to support a despair about resolving difficulties. Alternatively, the contest may be resolved tacitly through one of the contestants being silently awarded a laurel wreath denoting high community value, while the other collapses to a low value or comes to be persecuted as a community 'bad' object. In the latter case, morale in the community as a whole is maintained, although it may create crises of doubt in the demoted member of staff and in his minority of supporters; for example his small group, if he has any.

These staff problems often play on the patients' fears about the splits inside themselves, on their internal conflicts and contradictions. They come to feel supported in the view that problems cannot after all be resolved, that they cannot be spoken about. Rivalry, jealousy and other intense emotional experiences are confirmed as being insoluble. Patients can often feel involved in something so out of their control, while at the same time they may feel they have had some hand in causing it, that a cloud of helplessness settles more and more heavily over the community, and progressively over its activities.

The therapeutic use of this situation is difficult if the phantasy or the reality of staff difficulties cannot be explicitly acknowledged in words by the staff. However, it remains one of the single most important features of life in a therapeutic community. This community state touches on personal phantasies and anxieties of a very primitive kind – the fears about survival, madness and annihilation, and the intense forms of guilt and reparation. There is potential here for an important therapeutic experience for all or for very many of the community if it can be used (which is to say verbalized).

It is important to note that this community demoralization is not restricted to the community meeting but spreads over the rest of the activities of the community, leaving only pockets of sub-groups here and there free from its effect. This means that we cannot say complacently that even if the community itself is in a poor way, the patients can still rely on the special treatment situations retaining their therapeutic effectiveness: because they do not. In fact the relationships between the separate special treatment groups take on the same kinds of dissension, rivalry and splitting into idealized 'good' and 'bad' objects as those in which staff members are involved in the separate groups. The importance of the overall state of the organization cannot be ignored in its sub-groups (see for instance E 14.3 'The group carrying guilt', or E 14.8, 'The emotional hot potato').

Summary

The community accepts despairing people. The impact on the staff of people who put their last hopes in the hands of the staff is taxing. The acute sensitivity of the patients to the condition of the staff to whom they have turned so desperately reacts with the staff's sensitivity to being placed in the position of the patients' last hope. This is a recipe for much unspoken interchange about failure and doubt. It is, however, of central importance for the way in which the members feel the community organization to be succeeding – or failing.

9

Therapy and therapizing

Here we will exploit the concept of dramatization again in order to understand some features of the community processes in general. In example E 6.1 ('The man who thought he wanted to be himself'), the community meeting established a 'case-conference' kind of activity. Here is a similar example.

E 9.1 Therapizing the individual

After some initial announcements and a lethargic acceptance of a poor attendance, a brief disagreement between patients and staff grew up over whether Ian, who was about to lose his accommodation, should be admitted to the small in-patient unit for a while. The staff stuck to the view that this unit was not intended to deal with accommodation problems, and that Ian should not be admitted. The pressure for admission subsided and discussion began to fall flat. The staff had played into a dramatization – that the staff run the community here. The patients passively subsided indicating a resentful helplessness. It represented a relationship in which 'the staff make the decisions but they are not concerned with our problems'.

Shortly after this, Jenny focussed the meeting's attention on another patient, Kevin, who had told Jenny something earlier in the day. Kevin was invited to confide to the group and he said he had tried to gas himself the previous evening. He went on to talk about a fraught relationship with a current girlfriend. The meeting settled down to Kevin's case history and slowly prompted him with questions to try to draw out any lead which might be grasped. He was particularly elusive. The meeting, however, remained calmly persistent despite the signs of lethargy and boredom remaining within an overall atmosphere of depression.

It is not easy to convey the feeling of the way Kevin came across. He did not meet any expectation of how someone who had been attempting suicide only the night before should behave. He told us about a large part of himself which had been 'buried' – buried by the difficulties with his girlfriend. Slowly the theme turned to his destructiveness. Throughout, it was hard to get an impression of a man in love, or heartbroken or without violent passions. He appeared to be energetic in his talking, although perhaps it was rather forced. He tried hard to interest people and to make an impact on them. He did not succeed. And the meeting remained permanently in doubt about what it was that he wanted to impress on everybody. It had been rather an empty meeting which had focussed on a rather empty person.

The main verbal theme seemed to be the writing off of certain unwanted parts of the community (unwanted in the hospital in-patient unit).

Certain features of this meeting, however, had been repeated over and over again in recent weeks and had been discussed from time to time in staff meetings. Particular among these was the way in which the meeting focussed on one patient for a prolonged period of time, with other members asking him questions in a manner that had been described as 'playing therapist'.

In this kind of meeting Kevin got no reflection of himself since he got no affective response. He was not confronted verbally with other's views of himself. The continuous questioning was sympathetic and curious but uninformative. Nothing gave one the feel of a real person in relation to Kevin. It was a stalemate situation with a voyeuristic and remote tone, and it resembled many recent occasions.

At one level, one person was being offered a great deal of time and attention. On the other hand no useful psychotherapeutic work seemed to come from it. What we had before us was the appearance of psychotherapy – but not the substance.

In this instance, playing therapist was a dramatization of a situation in which help is not real help. Behind an empty caricature of therapy, which for his own reasons Kevin went along with, there was the resentful helplessness of the issue earlier in the meeting. Privately evolving attitudes on both the patients' side and the staff's were expressed in this indirect dramatized form.

These hidden attitudes were those of the early part of the meeting and were concerned with who made the decisions, and to whose benefit. The dramatization was a rehearsal in public of the current community divide between the two main sub-groups – patients and staff. A lethargic recognition of this split state, with no real commitment to work together, was then covered over by a whistling in the dark which had appearance of therapy – therapizing.

The meeting's defensiveness becomes clearer when seen in its context – a series of three meetings. Through this sequence the community anxieties emerge and there is a move towards verbal discovery.

E 9.2 Facing the worst

Meeting 1 was the one before the meeting described in example E 9.1 above. It was on a visitors' day. After a brief interest in who was absent (a denial of the presence of strangers) the meeting got into a non-progressing 'interviewing' style. In this case, patient Leo presented an appealing and placatory manner in the face of demanding and very intimate questioning which continued incessantly and insistently. At one point one of the visitors left without comment. The meeting became more excited as if provoked. It turned to vigorous and indignant protests about the intrusions of visitors whom they did not know. At one point I made a remark that the apparent concern for Leo was an attempt to get away from the clearly powerful anxiety about visitors. This was a clumsy way of expressing myself. It was unwise to overlook the possibility of genuine concern for Leo and my remark could have felt like belittling the whole of the first part of the meeting, and therefore belittling the efforts of all those who had tried in these peculiar circumstances to show their concern. It was also inaccurate to refer to 'anxiety' about visitors when the surface feeling was one of indignation. In both senses my remark 'overinterpreted' the meeting, and by not acknowledging the surface feelings first it made me just one of those staff who was out of touch. The outcome was that I was incorporated into a gathering dramatization of the hostility and divorce between patients and staff. The indignation towards the visitors for their intrusion changed now to the staff for their callous disregard of the patients and their feelings. The meeting ended in a high state of disturbance. Surprisingly, in the staff meeting afterwards some relief was expressed that the 'interviewing' type of therapizing had been disrupted – even though there was now a divorce of considerable magnitude between staff and patients. The hope was based on the view that any change is better than none at this stage.

Meeting 2 was described above. It is clear that the relief felt by the staff on the previous day was thoroughly premature. The meeting plunged more determinedly than ever into the therapizing interview. Perhaps, therefore, the staff were particularly hesitant about interrupting again on this day. After the meeting, the staff discussed together in some detail the kind of therapizing that was going on. Amid their own irritation, a common recognition began to develop. As a group they could at last share the feeling that they had not been very active or effective. Some painful discussion of this ensued. No very good solutions were found immediately and the meeting ended quietly with a sense of failure.

The following day, in meeting 3, the staff were more active. It started with the staff taking up an issue with one particular patient – significantly his passivity. But the discussion soon broadened out into a discussion about personal responsibility. It was thrown back and forth quite a lot between patients and staff. Such consciousness about the community processes continued to be discussed in subsequent meetings.

In the context of the longer term, the process towards discussing painful responsibility emerged from the dramatization of meeting 2. However, it required work by the staff. They had to face their own feelings of inadequacy. This was very important. The helplessness, emptiness and despair in meeting 2 attacked both sides of the community – and only through facing it could they come together again.

Determined therapizing

When the patients retreated into the resentful unhelped role, the staff were tempted to follow in the role of ever more insistent helpers.

Alarming scenes in ordinary mental hospitals in which staff are provoked into forcing vigorous treatments on to passive, resistant patients are related to this process. These are the acts of a desperate helper. He needs to know he is helping someone even if it is 'over their dead body'! Such cannot be quite the case in the therapeutic community – or can it? (see Clemental-Jones, 1985).

In fact considerable coercion can be brought to bear by staff, often in less overt ways. There are indeed various systems of social control within the therapeutic community (see Rapoport, 1960; Sharp, 1976). As members of a community staff must engage in the process of coping with non-conformity. Whether the community will be highly coercive with narrow limits of behaviour or highly permissive will depend on the most general common denominator for that community of people at that time. And members of staff are party to that.

In the name of therapy the staff member may find himself coercing the patient to 'be different'! Behaving and being are quite different modes of existence. Being oneself cannot really be controlled or censored in the way that behaving can. A person is what he is, however much he dislikes it.

To coerce someone to be a certain kind of person is to raise deep existential confusions that can only threaten their sense of identity (Bateson et al., 1956; Laing, 1960). This form of coercion is related to the entrapment of the individual in community roles in the dramatizations (for example, see E 2.2, 'The anti-scapegoat', and E 5.1, 'Splitting off a role'). Coercion to adopt the community defensiveness is treated by others, notably in Menzies' description (1960) of enforced introjection into the recruits to the nursing staff of a hospital (see chapters 5 and 13).

The group attack on awareness

It is true that staff and communities may be provoked to coerce treatment in this way, demanding that a patient 'be' different. Such change inside people, in their internal worlds, cannot be hurried – even to placate a staff member's anxious need to be helpful. The staff's urgency in this respect often leads to shortcuts being sought. In the next example the importance of the internal dimension of the person is denied and his behaviour is coerced without concern for what he 'is'.

A day community has to struggle to reconstitute itself again every morning. Some control of timing in the morning has to be established. With one particular patient lateness was simply defined as a bad habit and retraining was prescribed.

E 9.3 The bad-habit myth

A 25-year-old man came to the attention of the community for persistent oversleeping and late attendance. This was defined as bad, and a habit in need of breaking. The community then decided to admit him to the small in-patient unit in order to do this. In the unit his sleeping and working could be formed into new habits. Actually this failed. Although he could then wake up at the right time, he did so only while staying in the hospital. When he left the in-patient unit and resumed as a day patient, he reverted immediately to the old pattern.

He was himself distressed that such an expensive treatment (full-time nursing care) should be offered him for the simple task of breaking a bad habit – especially when it became a wasted expense. In fact his oversleeping was an actively motivated symptom. It had a meaning in the totality of his life. He was deeply concerned at wasting expensive resources in general. He had wasted not only his life and the hospital's efforts, but also the university education which his working-class family had put such a high value on (higher than their son's happiness, so he believed).

In this example the person at the focus of attention was required to act through a dramatization which asserted certain assumptions about what is wrong with patients (that this comes down to bad habits) and how to put them right. Such a set of assumptions avoided the work of gaining insight and denied the internal world. This was a radical but momentary departure from the normal psychotherapeutic stance of this community. Rationalized as behaviour modification therapy, in this community it was actually a defensive move. Like other forms of coercion and discipline it defended against the urgent need for the staff to have quick and reassuring results. From the patient's viewpoint, the promise of a simpler and easier treatment could gratefully be accepted. Collectively, there might have been the wish to avoid the painful examination of a sense of waste. At this time the nursing authorities in the National Health Service were questioning the economic and therapeutic viability of this in-patient unit. By the usual happy chance the community was able to push to the fore a master experienced at dealing with demands of this kind for quick results.

Redefining symptoms as bad habits is quite common. Cooper (1967, pp. 101-2) noted the same attitude to sleeping late. I am not at this point questioning whether behaviour modification is effective. The issue here is that the decision to try it in this community was not typical and emerged from strong emotional forces amongst the staff and patients. This kind of redirection is strongly suggestive of unconscious defensiveness. I shall term it 'task drift'.

Once the task of the community or of any part of it has been defined, it should be clear when one of these tell-tale drifts from the task has occurred (see Rice, 1963). However, in practice it is not quite so easy. As we now know, people can get caught up blindly in community processes. The adoption of a distorted task is just another effect of a dramatization. Once people are caught up in it they often lose sight of the defined task. The dramatization provides an alternative view of the community. So 'therapizing' is a dramatization that involves a drift away from the real task of exploring the individuals' experiences of the community. The defensive nature of this is explored further in Chapter 11 (see especially Figs. 11.4 and 11.5).

Flight into activity

Similar to the surreptitious change of the task is another movement in the community process: the flight into activity. It is similar to dramatization, and again it is devoted to externalizing and denying internal situations. Like the sudden adoption of a behaviour modification approach, flight into activity is a total immersion in physical occupations. Reflection on experience and emotional states is squeezed out by a productive activity.

E 9.4 Accommodating patients

Community meetings had for several days repeatedly returned to Ivy and the practicalities of finding accommodation for her. As the discussion went on, and the days went on without the patient finding anywhere to live, frustration with the topic mounted. There seemed to be an unspoken appeal – 'we never get anywhere in the discussions in these meetings'. The implication was that the members were frustrated because the community had not been able to achieve any practical result. However, it can also be seen as the dramatization of a relationship which needed verbalizing. It did in fact turn out that the repetitious movement towards some action on accommodation was doomed because it was being used to express other feelings. In fact the problem at that moment was to accommodate the patients' feelings (perhaps the staff's, too).

Ivy's housing problem expressed the failure to contain the distress; and then on top of that the mounting distress at the failure to recognize the feelings about the failure to contain.

This flight into activity in the external world may be quite productive in itself. But if the results of the activity are evaluated only as activity people often feel patronized. In a therapeutic community there is plenty of external activity in the psychotherapeutic setting because the members have to arrange things and look after the community. Activity can then easily cloak a defensiveness. The practical needs of the community momentarily become hooks to hang a dramatization on. Because the defensiveness hides a store of urgent feelings, the activity is intensely energetic and driving. Yet a price has to be paid, and it is paid in the distortion of reality, especially the reality of the emotional internal world.

In society at large vast quantities of energy may be devoted to highly active pursuits based on very flimsy evidence of relevance to the real situation – for example, wars. This energy can keep groups and communities solidly together and frantically active. Its source may be a cohesive force derived from the need to cope with common frustration and feelings in the life of the group.

'Doing something useful' is not enough in itself, however energetically pursued. It must be a realistic contribution to the primary task. A therapeutic community must confront and learn from the frustrations and tensions created by living together. Nevertheless, most members will at times dedicate themselves to defensive evasions of the task. Efforts to divert and 'do something useful' will mount with an imperative force. The task then drifts and the community has made a collective attack on its own awareness of the internal world.

It is not all that difficult to get a therapeutic community to be active. Many people can proudly claim a radical change in ward atmosphere away from the 'warehousing of vegetables' towards active rehabilitation of the old chronic long-stay in-mates. Miller and Gwynne (1972) describe the grisly task facing the staff of homes for the permanently disabled. They show how cultures grow up for the defensive needs of staff. The task of care is diverted into either enforcing total dependence on the part of the inmates or conversely establishing a painfully over-ambitious independence. The benefits of these kinds of regimes have to be cautiously assessed against those of a realistic task with limited aims.

Occupational therapists no longer promote activity for the sake of it. For the therapeutic community the task must be therapeutic first and active only as appropriate (see Christian and Hinshelwood, 1979).

Summary

The despair that there never will be adequate help is very prevalent amongst a community of people who have broken down. On a community scale this is often dealt with by means of collective dramatizations, one example of which is a simulated form of therapy which I have termed therapizing. It dangerously offers opportunities for evasion to both staff and patients. Two related kinds of evasion also are task drift and flight into action.

10

Failure and the ideal

By definition, community members have suffered a more or less complete breakdown in their ability to manage their lives or to achieve. For whatever reasons, they are failures in society. And whatever their political views about the value of contemporary society, this sense of failure has ground its way deep into their personalities.

Thereafter, at least one of the immediate demands will be that the therapeutic community should contain that sense of failure. As we shall see later (in chapter 19 on the community personality as container), there are alternative methods for helping members to cope with their own feelings of having failed at what is important to them. Usually, the first demand is to get rid of the feeling altogether. Usually, someone else is supposed to feel a failure instead. That person may be someone outside the community. More often the staff are introduced to the feeling by being made to feel it directly for the patients.

Communities which are swamped by feelings of failure may go through periods of considerable fear for their survival, often collectively projecting into external authority the view that they are worthless. In some instances, external authority has closed a few down – perhaps in a collusive dramatization with the community itself. Certainly some instances suggest that the authority only acts to confirm the loss of heart within the community itself (Foster, 1979). The helplessness and failure can come to have a convincing reality for the community. However, in large measure it is an externalization, for we have many patients collected together for whom failure, helplessness and hopelessness are basic ingredients of their internal worlds. Therapists come to know these feelings very directly:

> *I finally had to conclude that feelings of helplessness and*
> *hopelessness were part of the burden I had to bear as a therapist,*
> *and that I was not alone in experiencing them. I also began to see*
> *that these feelings came up with greatest intensity in certain*
> *kinds of patients who had certain things in common. And, in*
> *spite of my best intentions, I found myself repeatedly hopeless,*
> *helpless and furious.* (Adler, 1972)

Not only do such patients repeatedly reduce their therapists to impotent defeat in the process of repeating these convictions in the transference, but they then end up collected together in institutions such as a therapeutic community.

Patients come to experience the community as a failure, whatever it may be like. In addition, they can bring their therapists to the same point of desperation. Staff and patients can get into a downward spiral of pessimism about the community and about the future of treatment for the individual patients. In order to preserve some confidence in the community both staff and patients have to take desperate measures. Staff may impulsively push the failure back on to the individual patients — 'they are the real failures and that's that'.

E 10.1 The reign of terror

During a period in which the mood of the day community was dominated by the holidays of the senior staff, there were a number of discharges. On his return from his holiday, one of the psychiatrists was told – 'Everyone is still alive! But because the community has been tightening up in terms of contracts and attendance, a lot of people have been discharged.' In fact, one after another had been discharged because they could not 'use the hospital'. This diagnosis was connected with a strong demand to conform to rather strict criteria for using the hospital which included not just good attendance, but that members should express themselves adequately in words when called upon to do so. Some sort of myth was gathering momentum, such as – 'you can't know anything about anyone unless he tells you in so many words'. Members were also required to show an attitude of enduring willingness, even when expressing distaste, unwillingness or anger. For a group of disturbed people, verbal expression of what was unconscious was, at the least, difficult. We have seen the resort to dramatization. Often the situation was felt to be hopeless. Any such community could not help but find a succession of suitable people for failing these criteria. A 'reign of terror' ensued. A quarter of the membership had been discharged as failures – the numbers fell from 36 to 27.

This did not happen lightly, for there was considerable anxiety through identifying with those discharged. Guilt centred around the question whether there was some pathological dynamic going on that nobody was effectively managing to control. The fear was of something omnipotently damaging which people also felt some responsibility for.

The return of some of the senior staff brought the community to a dead stop. There were overwhelming feelings of passivity and inhibition. A process of dividing the patients into senior members and the rest was immediately superseded by all patients becoming very junior on the return of the senior staff. The decline in morale was complete.

What seemed to have arisen was a difficulty in facing the fact that 'things could be difficult'. When difficulties arose they were discharged – in the form of a patient. Yet the problem then was that they did not fully disappear. What the patient was made to represent remained after he had gone. Added to the vestiges of his departure was an accumulating sense that something must be amiss if so many were being discharged. The 'bit of difficulty' that had been discharged returned with a vengeance. The difficulty was now augmented by the sense of guilt and failure. The next discharge became a new attempt to deal with this, but brought a similar return. A vicious circle was started up, gripping everyone in an unhappy process which felt as though it had got quite out of hand.

The process was overlaid by a rational approach based on some idea of 'using the hospital', which involved speaking one's feelings and pain directly to the community. The difficulty with using this approach was that by definition patients are unable to verablize. They can only dramatize; and in a helpless way many became agents colluding in their own discharge.

The move to recognize senior patients as a category apart failed. Although it had succeeded in 'getting something done' (the discharges), there were none who really wanted to be responsible for it. The greater the effort to control conformity, the more the community felt as though things were getting out of hand. The only means of extricating the community from this disastrous progress was to embody a magical leadership in the returning staff. The interacting effects of failure, guilt, responsibility, omnipotence and magic are important and are summarized below in chapter 11 (Fig. 11.2, 'Success slides further out of reach'). Failure led to the hope for something magically omnipotent and to a delusion that the community was just as magical as is needed. When delusion burst, guilt was added to the sense of failing. Responsibility acquired a crippling weight as it became increasingly a responsibility for a hopeless failure requiring an ever more magical agent to correct it. Problems of this kind reflect back on the staff. For them, the community represents hopes for their future career and some fulfilment in life. Confidence against personal insecurities is bolstered by becoming a member of the staff of a successful community. That personal support sags with the community. For some members of staff, their own early feelings of helplessness and failure are hidden behind ambitious and omnipotent notions of curing, healing and changing people. They can often put aside disillusionment with themselves by sharing disillusionment over the community; by blaming a particular person – either deviant or patient or dominant leader; or by giving up the therapeutic community method as no use after all. These ploys attempt to leave the sense of failure behind.

The therapeutic community blueprint

The exquisite sense of failure is connected with the interplay of the omnipotent needs of patients and the omnipotent phantasies that staff entertain about themselves. Such a 'neurotic fit' is always going wrong. If it is not repeatedly acknowledged and pointed out, grave and distressing processes like the 'reign of terror' take over the community.

One important method members may use to extricate themselves from the distress of helplessness and failure is to take refuge in an attitude of withdrawal from the experience. Some staff, like patients, may leave the community altogether. Another possibility is to withdraw emotionally.

Patients may adopt this passive attitude by inviting a dose of treatment. Staff, too, may 'prescribe a course of therapeutic community treatment' as if it were a drug. The therapeutic community is then regarded as a cure process which operates upon patients in a passive sojourn through there. The idea is that some proper organization, planned in advance according to some blueprint, will be established and set in motion. Good results can then automatically be expected to flow from this social machinery.

This is the social engineering approach. Its straightforwardness might make it worth considering if it were possible. There cannot in fact be a set of ingredients that make up a 'standard therapeutic community'. Nor can it be administered to a patient like a drug. This is a wholly defensive illusion. Like all psychological defences it persuasively blinds those involved in it. There are many efforts to define what a proper therapeutic community should be, but they are very varied (see Kennard, 1983). The only practical ideal is that there should be no ideal.

The community exists to find its own solutions to the problems it confronts. Thus there are some tasks the community must organize itself for. How it does so will be the idiosyncratic expression of each community.

The organization that grows up in a community does so as the outcome of decisions about the problems that the community has faced. As solutions of past problems, each community organization has cryztallised out from its own history. As a working organization designed to face present problems and adapt to them, the community has only a certain principle for guiding the relationship between the individual and the community. That principle is focussed towards confronting the individuality of each person.

The therapeutic community attitude is directly opposed to the social engineering approach. Subjecting a patient to a cure process is in direct conflict with living through with somebody their experience of their own worst fears. To 'engineer' an ideal therapeutic community is to deny the process of change and progress of the individuals who make up the changing living community (see Jones, 1982).

It denies that the community 'is' the individuals who make it up. There is a divorce between the two, and curiosity is stifled. The relationship between the individual and the community is over-looked, primarily to avoid the pain of that relationship when it feels hopeless. This also intensifies a split actually within the individual. When he projects something of himself into the community it is lost, because as part of the community it becomes a fundamentally separate thing (see also Hinshelwood, 1983). The identity of the individual becomes stripped down – just as occurred in the old institutionalizing process that the therapeutic community reacted against (Barton, 1959; Goffman, 1961). The flexible interplay of projective and introjective identifications is disrupted by a contin-uous overbalance on the side of projection.

This process may suit the patient in his search for relief from his own painful internal world. If the institution offers this kind of divorce from himself he may feel better. However he ends up dependent in an oddly tenacious way on an institution which has captured major parts of his own identity. He remains tied to an institution which is in possession of a part of himself he is divorced from!

The institutionalization of the old mental hospitals is a process sickly adhered to by defensive patients and staff (Hinshelwood, 1979). In short, patients lose that part of themselves which makes them totally hopeless; the staff withdraw from contact with the hopelessness; both come to believe it is too much to be tolerated.

The polemic here against the notion of the ideal community draws on this book's descriptions of the defensive manoeuvring of communities. However, there are other pressures from outside which demand a standard blueprint. Funding authorities, particularly, prefer to look at just this sort of engineered plan that can be quantified, costed and eventually scientifically measured (see Man-ning, 1979). The medical model of professional diagnosis and prescription often gets entangled with the therapeutic community merely through proximity, and modes of thinking are carried across by patients as well as administrators, and by the medically trained professionals.

Summary

There are many ways of attempting to avoid the sense of failure and despair through dramatizations. One major form is to export it. An illustration of the attempt to 'discharge' it in the form of patients showed how the community could decimate itself to an extreme degree. Another method is to mechanize the process, to engineer from an ideal therapeutic community blueprint, and then process individuals without acknowledging and living with their experiences.

11

Morale and demoralization

To be effective, morale has to be sustained on the basis of a cruelly accurate appreciation of reality. In the therapeutic community it is the reality of what can be done for patients in treatment, and in particular for the present patients.

Morale is the capacity of the group or community to maintain a belief in itself on this realistic basis. Group beliefs are notoriously capricious. Classical experiments in social psychology were preoccupied with this. Sherif and Sherif (1961), Asch (1952), Mayo (1933) and Milgram (1963) represent this founding urge of social psychology. Asch showed that individuals are dominated more by group pressures than by their own judgements. He demonstrated that a person on his own could not stand up against the group opinion even when it contradicted his own senses – even when the judgement was something as objective as the length of a line. Milgram, yet more frighteningly, showed the willingness of experimental subjects to administer dangerous levels of electrical shocks to people, when under coercive social pressure. Festinger (1950) and Festinger *et al.*, (1950) emphasized that the influence of the group is much greater still when the matter is one of belief rather than objective judgements.

Morale is more stable when there is an objective, measurable output such as from a factory, or an annual profit. It is understandable that conventional psychiatric practice looks for objective and measurable outputs like the removal of symptoms, behaviour modification, relapse rates, or even falling bed numbers within an institution. These are frequently-used props against an erratic morale. When the end result is something as intangible as a change in an individual's personality (especially the unconscious part of his personality), the group beliefs will clearly be susceptible to volatile changes. What are the influences that effect this system of group beliefs?

In this chapter we will look at one category of factors: those emotional ones which have already emerged as dramatizations. They distort a belief in the effectiveness of the community, into either an omnipotent, or a failing community.

Morale and the demoralized organization

Rapoport (1956) noticed cyclical variations in the cohesiveness of a community and in the individual's allegiance to the community. He termed this 'oscillation' – an unhappy analogy with machinery. Early forms of powered engines varied widely in speed and power sometimes said to 'hunt' a stable state. In spite of this graceless allusion to engineering, social organizations have equally problematic dynamics. As we have seen, they can go hunting after strange and unrealistic ends.

The task, and feelings about its attainability, have a profound effect on the members of an organization. Menzies emphasized the importance of clarity in defining what the realistic function is:

> *Quite simply, unless the members of the institution know what it is they are supposed to be doing, there is little hope of their doing it effectively and getting adequate satisfaction in doing so. Lack of such definition is likely to lead to personal confusion in the members of the institution, to inter-personal and inter-group conflict and to other undesirable institutional phenomena.*
>
> (1979, p. 197)

This is an apt comment on experiences met within large mental hospitals, and it serves as an exemplary account of a demoralized institution (Hinshelwood, 1979). Where there is conflict between multiple alternative functions, or when insufficient resources are provided, the individuals will suffer (Bott, 1976). The cost is always felt in terms of job satisfaction and working relations with colleagues. Staff feel inadequate, having an uneasy sense of failing in their job, often finding it hard to put a finger on exactly where they fail, especially if the functions have drifted in unconscious ways due to unconsciously driven evasions. The end result is conscious enough when they feel inadequate and dissatisfied.

In the course of time such uncertainty eats into the confidence of the staff collectively. They may begin to lose sight of their own roles within the organization. Eventually they may look around for roles that they feel enhance their own sense of adequacy and value. At the same time they will, in turn, feel encroached upon by others similarly looking for a sense of adequacy and value.

Friction and this special form of rivalry come to the fore. The staff no longer feel securely embedded in the smooth functioning of the organization. Much of their own attempts to enhance their sense of adequacy relies on denigrating the efforts of others within the organizations. They do not support each other. Instead they belittle others' efforts and by so doing they suppose themselves to be better. The member attempts to lift himself up by the boot-straps.

The continuous mutual denigration brings others down too. The general atmosphere of belittling criticism leads to a general feeling of going unappreciated—just when the need is for mutual support. Lack of appreciation leads to grudging hostility and an enhanced denigration. Each person is driven to work more for himself than for the organization. He is the only one able to appreciate what he actually achieves.

His self-appreciation is further driven by the urgent need to protect his own psychological survival. The demoralization of the organization and personal despair go hand in hand.

From this personal predicament attacks begin to be made on the institution itself. It is bitterly criticized for being too slack and inefficient, and also for being too arbitrary and dictatorial. A hopelessness develops, a collective shrugging of the shoulders owing to no-one feeling they are listened to or supported. There is a kind of hatred of the job, since anything which goes wrong plays on a personal sense of inadequacy and insignificance. In particular, patients who do not within this ethos confirm for the nurse that he is valued will come to be hated by the nurse for reminding him of his own uncertainty about himself. Verbal and sometimes physical attacks may result from the nurse's anguish. Administrators, too, are hated if they do not confirm a person's value by jumping to meet his demands and granting him the resources he expects at once. The administrators in turn are overwhelmed by demands to make people feel important and to do so by gratifying demands.

One dilemma for the individual in such an organization is that there is not really felt to be anything to form an allegiance with. There is merely a gap, an emptiness at the core of things. In such a gap it is a matter of everyone for himself. Yet this is not the freedom of the permissive community, but a spurious autonomy. In the ragged remnants of organization the individual has a wide scope to do what he wants, yet he receives no recognition and only by chance will his activities contribute to the whole.

These extreme states of demoralization are very difficult for members to cope with. Although typical of traditional mental hospitals, this spiralling fragmentation together with accelerating despair and insecurity can be seen at times in most therapeutic communities. Much of the rest of this book is concerned with these important community states.

The individual has various methods for surviving these conditions. First, a characteristic way is the creation of personal empires, autonomous departments or sub-groupings within the organization. To enhance his personal security, the individual gathers around him what he can. In such groups, as we shall see in part IV, odd things happen as one sub-group tries to preserve its own importance for itself at the expense of another sub-group. Secondly, in other areas, for instance in clinical work, there is an inappropriately aggressive pursuit of the hospital purpose. We have seen the creation of pseudo-therapeutic kinds of meetings (E 9.1, 'Therapizing the individual'). Thirdly, many people disengage, and without leaving altogether they blunt their own distress with distance – witness the defensive blueprint-maker in the last chapter. Others with great humour convert their own frustrations into sensational stories for the amusement of friends and acquaintances. This may provide good after-dinner conversation. A variant of this posture of one foot out of the grave, is to take an academic stance and write thoughtful articles, papers or books into which are poured the now neutralized and distant frustration and insecurity. Fourthly, a further step from the immediate present is to engage in some political activity. In this move, people become indignant rather than amused, and demand that something should be done. Lack of clear leadership can provoke, through exasperation and some intimidation, a particularly rigid form of unionized protest to substitute for cohesiveness. Fifthly, the last main alternative is to seek some therapeutic way out. That would mean facing the experience rather than evading it.

Individuals are especially sensitive to the state of the organization they are identified with. A group, a community, an institution or an industrial concern each demands an allegiance of some kind. The members respond with varying kinds of identification. In the demoralized organization, the allegiance is of a special and inconsistent kind. Often the confidence to move on has faltered. The members remain only to develop a mateyness amongst themselves based on slighting references to the organization and its performance. There may be an affectionate scorn for what goes wrong, as if typical – and only to be expected. For the most part, this is laced with a hûmour which makes the most denigrating attitudes apparently harmless. However, these jokes make sure that every failing of the organization is common knowledge. The humour makes it hard for the gravity of the situation to be shared. It is an intimidating hegemony which prevents individuals from standing out against the common humorous attitudes. Each person is obliged to follow suit with further stories. All members alike share the collective despair, but collectively shrug it off as a joke.

Sometimes the organization becomes, momentarily, the hoped-for omnipotent answer to everyone's prayers; but the mood does not last. This kind of confidence in the organization can be a mere bubble. It is no real answer to the morale problem. The bursting of the bubble once again sets in motion the splitting and the mutual projection systems which have operated all along. Morale sets off on another downward spin.

The two roots of morale

The failing of the organization touches upon the awful personal phantasies of fragmentation and falling apart. It would seem that morale has two basic ingredients – a belief in the integrity of the community and a belief in its effectiveness.

Integrity: This means here the shared belief in the wholeness of the community. Rapoport noticed that the oscillations in his community were connected with important community members leaving (this is reflected in the example in the next chapter E 12.1 'Rescuing morale').

The community may also be riven by internal divisions which are very fragmenting. Some of the dramatizations we have seen concern intense splits between sub-groups working against each other. These divisions arise as subjective experiences in the sub-groups involved, but they achieve a kind of objectivity, because the beliefs of one sub-group about another do actually come about under the pressure of the other's beliefs and projections.

Integrity involves the feeling that the membership is clearly demarcated and stable – and that the separate groups within the community are working together. In contast to this is the belief in the fragmentation of the community.

Effectiveness: Closely related to the question of integrity is the set of beliefs about the community's ability to do what it sets out to do, beliefs which are beset by strong emotional forces. The work may be conceived in highly unrealistic terms based on the individuals' despair. The community has constantly to clarify the scale of the task that can be attained – even if it does not meet expectations. It has to prevent task drift (see E 9.3, 'The bad-habit myth') which moves the work away from something which seems too difficult towards some other easier but less relevant task. Usually the task becomes the evasion of feelings about an ineffective community.

Figure 11.1 shows the interrelations of these influences. The top of the diagram shows a vicious circle which feeds into itself. If the integrity is threatened (position 1) a belief in the effectiveness of the organization suffers (position 2). Going back to the early example of the suffering community (E 3.1), the integrity was threatened by a doctor becoming depressed. The internal boundary between staff and patients was suddenly breached. The result was that there were considerable doubts about the effectiveness of the community to contain madness. The loss of belief in the organization was sufficiently intense for defences to leap into operation, and the doubts were expressed as dramatizations (position 3). Projections expressed in the

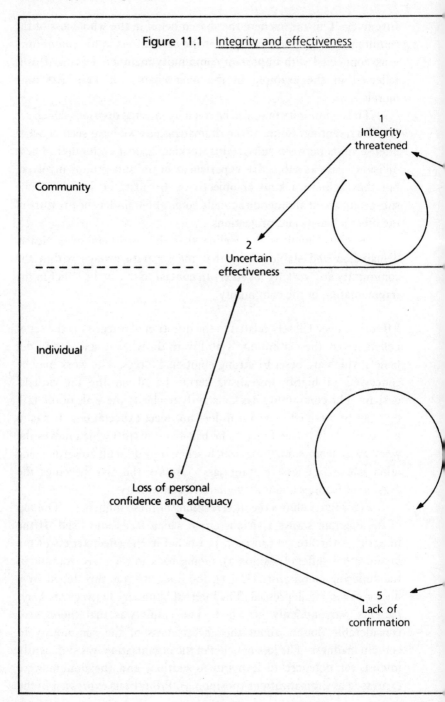

Figure 11.1   Integrity and effectiveness

Community

Individual

1
Integrity
threatened

2
Uncertain
effectiveness

6
Loss of personal
confidence and adequacy

5
Lack of
confirmation

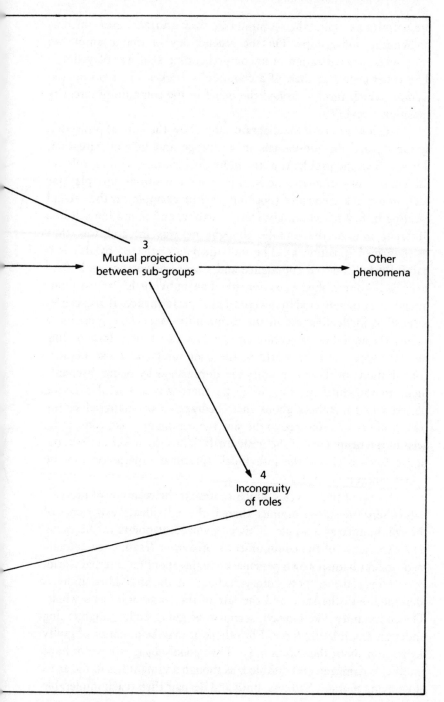

3
Mutual projection
between sub-groups

Other
phenomena

4
Incongruity
of roles

dramatizations split the community even further into uncomprehending sub-groups. On the second day of that example an entrenched dramatization of uncomprehending staff was played out. The experience was then of a community broken up into opposed factions which further eroded the belief in the community integrity (position 1 again).

The lower part of the diagram shows how the mutual projection systems place the individuals in a strange and difficult situation. These reflect the problems of the individual compressed into roles in the community dramatizations. The roles the sub-groups play for each other lack congruity (position 4). For example, in the second meeting in E 3.1 Richard got Harriet wrong, and found himself in a different role to the one he thought he was in, and was thus disconfirmed (position 5). The individuals are affected by this in a painful way. Personal confidence and a sense of potency and effectiveness is diminished (position 6). The individuals' lack of confidence may be reflected in lowered actual performance. It also causes a sense of ineffectiveness in the community as a whole (position 2 again) through the projection of the phantasies of a fragmenting internal world into the world of the community; and also because contributions to the community are diminished by being disconfirmed. In the third meeting in E 3.1 there was a woeful dialogue between two members about their bedraggled or shattered family backgrounds – a reference to the way the community had come to be seen in the phantasies of the individuals. Thus the lower cycle in the figure feeds back via the individuals' personal experience into the upper community cycle.

On top of these cycles which represent the relations of individuals in separate sub-groupings, there is the individuals' experience of the community as a whole. This is involved at points in the cycle. The experience of the community as broken or fragmented actually feeds the individual's own personal anxieties about his internal world.

It may arouse persecutory feelings in the individual if he is identified with the state and the fate of the community as a whole. The community, like himself, seems to be going under, fragmenting under an annihilating force. For others, it may be a matter of guilty depression about the community. This 'good' object, source of hope and life, is damaged and disabled; as though an infant lies in the arms of its dying mother. Sadness, guilt and despair then reach intolerable proportions. In both cases escape is sought in primitive defences – individual or collective.

Omnipotence and failure again

The following example is one of the community rendered powerless.

E 11.1 The hamstrung community

Kathleen decided to leave the small group which she had been attending for a number of months. She did so at a time when others were also attending irregularly. There remained only two members of that small group, as well as the two staff members. Some pressure was put on her to continue to attend, but without effect. In order to regenerate the small group it was decided to put in several new people as they arrived.

Consequently, on arrival, Lily was assigned. However, before she had started in the group she requested a week off because relatives were coming to stay in London and needed to be looked after. The community meeting discussed this and seemed powerless to do anything but agree. The meeting could not say 'no'. After Lily had been attending for some two weeks she complained to the community meeting that she could not attend one of the small group sessions each week. She had an afternoon course at college. She claimed that she had agreed to come to the community in the first place only on condition that she could attend her college. This had been agreed at the outset. Therefore it was the community's responsibility to sort this out.

At this stage the community was in such a desultory condition that it could not sort it out. The problem seemed insoluble; like the sense of an insoluble difficulty which so many people carried inside them. What was required was a correspondingly omnipotent problem solver. Despair drenched the community. It was simply agreed after a short and desultory discussion that Lily should leave the small group on these occasions. This would of course be a further disturbance to a small group already in trouble.

Undeniably the problem presented to the community by Lily was a difficult one. The undertaking given before Lily was admitted to the community might in other circumstances have been acceptable, but in this case it became a clash of loyalties. In its demoralized state, the community was only able to resort to the line of least resistance – acquiescing to the demands of the patient herself. The effect on the small group was recognized but discounted. The effect on the community procedures was not investigated. Just as important, the relationship between Lily and the community was only tentatively mentioned before being put easily on one side.

Lily dramatized a relationship – passing responsibility over to the community in a most challenging way. A crippling burden of responsibility was indeed a community issue at the time – although in very early stages of being tackled.

At this point it was too much for the community. Every care was taken to avoid hurting Lily's feelings. In itself this might have been laudable – except that the community perhaps, and the small group certainly, were damaged. The task of examining Lily's relationship with the community was also damaged. The inability of a community of some forty people to stand up to the demands – and the projections – of one determined member is remarkable. One has the impression of the community being held to ransom. By passing over responsibility Lily aroused a persecuting sense of guilt in others. To avoid this, and to appease Lily, the community as a whole was offered as a kind of sacrifice. If they say 'no' the members immediately become accused of the most outrageous act against humanity. This typical dramatization in which a poor individual is apparently helplessly victimized by an unfeeling community is only equalled by the reality of the situation in which an adroit and ruthless patient can hamstring the community.

The communal apathy accepted that personal demands overrode everything else (see E 7.2, 'The ruling mafiosi'). The task had drifted to an unrealistic and defensive demand on the community, and the community suffered a further increased belief in its ineffectiveness. This is illustrated as a rolling cycle in figure 11.2. Because the task seemed so difficult and the community so puny, any success seemed to require omnipotent efforts. To pin Lily down to a responsibility for her own choices and the consequences for others seemed to ask too much and to cast doubt on the ability of the community (position 1).

The result was an easy drift into something which at first promised total success – satisfying Lily's request (position 2). In fact such an easy way out led to more community trouble (position 3) and a vicious circle was completed as the demoralization intensified (position 4). Success slipped further out of reach making the task drift towards more short-term achievements.

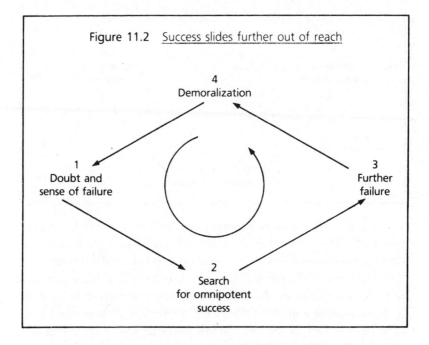

Figure 11.2   Success slides further out of reach

Searching for immediate success to counteract the sagging morale entailed a progressive lessening of the appreciation of reality. In the example the reality became restricted to Lily's demands matched by a defensive belief in the goodness and effectiveness of the community.

A similar unreal idealization was illustrated in example E 5.4, 'The community as paradise'. This myth led to another vicious circle (Fig. 11.3). As position 1 it led to the determination to ignore any unpleasantness (position 2) and reached a stage when the staff actually thought that the patients were harmed by too much softness (position 3). So they toughened up (position 4)! All they achieved was to reinforce the myth (position 1 again).

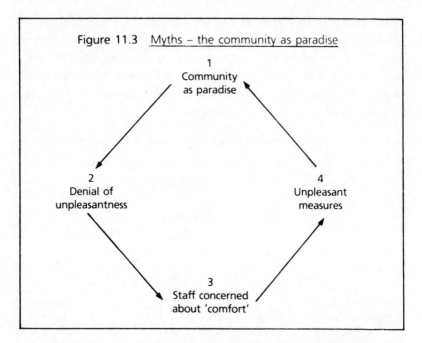

Figure 11.3   Myths – the community as paradise

Figure 11.4 shows the general pattern of the search to be good at something. More often than not a drifting task fails simply because the community does not deliver the goods and so belief falls further.

However, communities may survive on polarized attitudes (splitting). These emphasize the goodness of the community in opposition to the badness of something else – drug treatments, or some other kind of institution such as the local mental hospital. This may be founded on no evidence at all; or reality may provide some evidence on which beliefs can be hung. The community can seem to succeed at last. It is different and better than some other inferior treatment or institution.

Task drift is involved in similar self-idealizing cycles (see Fig. 11.5). In the example of the reign of terror (E 10.1), the community took one of its subsidiary tasks – discharging – to great lengths in order to demonstrate an effectiveness and thus raise morale by making the community seem potent, and by making some patients feel senior. Discharging is undeniably part of the community task, but in this case it was raised to be the overall task. Having hit upon an operation that the community did succeed at, it was increasingly difficult to get the situation under control in spite of the nagging doubts that something was wrong.

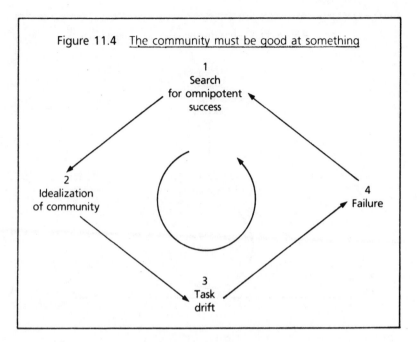

Figure 11.4   The community must be good at something

Finally, Figure 11.6 shows how the split between the therapeutic community and some other group is mutually used. In example E 14.1, 'The TC ward', one ward in a large mental hospital adopted therapeutic community principles. But this became an opportunity used by all wards to enhance a belief in their superiority. The therapeutic community ward felt it was the best just by virtue of being a therapeutic community (position 1), but this threatened the other wards (position 2), who responded by denigrating the therapeutic community ward (position 3). This emphasized the difference (position 4), which the therapeutic community ward could then rationalize as evidence for their superiority – because they stood out, they were better (back to position 1). Many other examples could be formulated in diagram form – for example, E 9.1, 'Therapizing the individual'; as could a lot of the problematic relations between staff and patients described in chapter 8, which discussed staff as the transference object.

This method of dealing with demoralized feelings by seeking an easier task is known as task drift, and is especially noticeable where the primary (or proper) task is obscure and not easily defined in operational terms, or where the resources for achieving the task are not

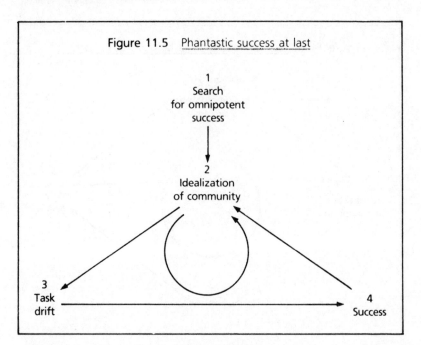

Figure 11.5   Phantastic success at last

sufficient to meet the needs of the staff (see Menzies, 1979; Hood, 1985).

The next chapter will apply these cycles to an extended example illustrating a prolonged period of demoralization and how the community worked its way out of the situation.

Summary

Personal despair and despair about the organization go hand in hand. The experience of working in a demoralized organization is not very different from the experience of the patient who has come to the end of the road with his life. When it seems that nothing further can be done to improve things, there is the expectation that only an omnipotent helper will do the trick. The omnipotent helper never exists – all resources and skills are limited. For both patients and staff this creates situations which it is tempting to evade rather than face. The formal analyses of the state of demoralization schematize how dramatizations feed a vicious circle which leads to a self-defeating state of demoralization – a demoralization trap. While remaining in the dramatizing

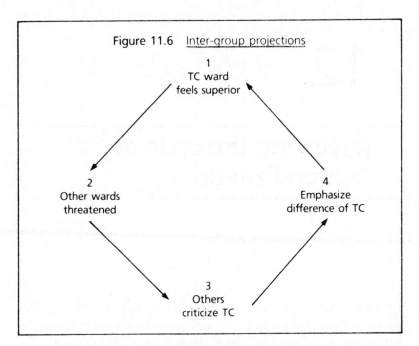

Figure 11.6   Inter-group projections

1
TC ward
feels superior

2
Other wards
threatened

4
Emphasize
difference of TC

3
Others
criticize TC

mode, the roles and relationships enacted will concern the despairing search for omnipotent help; they create situations which lead to even more despair.

12

Reversing the cycle of demoralization

I shall attempt here to tease out some of the characteristic reverberations between patients and staff, amongst patients, amongst staff, or between other sub-groups. The example is necessarily detailed.

E 12.1 Rescuing morale

For a prolonged period, demoralization within the community was expressed in long silences, desultory, short-lived conversations and a pervading sense of purposelessness in the community meetings. Brief respite usually took the form of incisive comments from Nelly, a member of staff, who happened to be leaving shortly. Usually at this point one particular patient or other was put on the spot. Other comments would then be expressed in a neutral sort of way. There would be a tone of unexpressed but polarized resentment between the community and the staff member leaving.

There were actually two members of staff leaving at this time, Nelly and Nat. The whole staff group felt itself to be in disarray, the prime difficulty being the apparent reluctance of other members of staff to come forward to offer themselves to fulfil the commitments of those leaving. It was clear that this was partly an indirect expression of resentment against Nat and Nelly.

The staff were saying in effect, 'don't think that your places are worth filling, we'll do everything differently and better when you've gone'. In response Nat and Nelly tended to express all the anxiety about what would happen after they had gone, and to draw attention to the dismal state of affairs, as if remarking, 'you can't be trusted to be left with the community in your hands' (see below Fig. 12.1, 'The unsure staff').

In the community, the inter-group interactions were somewhat different. For the patients, the staff were in disarray and this contributed to a profound sense of insecurity and despair. One could say that there was a tendency to see the main emotional difficulties as lying within the staff, and this was not entirely unrealistic.

On the other hand, for the staff, the disturbance was regarded as naturally lying with the patient side of the community. Individuals were constantly put on the spot to represent this – 'the patients are anxious, irresponsible, depressed', etc. All of this was probably true enough, although the staff were tempted to take this opportunity for projection (compare E 5.3, 'A collective projection').

The staff problem at this time was to redistribute amongst other members the responsibilities of the two who were leaving. Irresponsibility, or fear of failing at responsibilities, was being projected so that individual patients came to represent it for the staff. For the patients it was the staff who were depleted, anxious, and irresponsibly abandoning the community. Neither side seemed aware of the others' assumptions. In so far as communications from either were based on these separate assumptions, they could not be accurately received, and were only reinterpreted on the other side in the light of other assumptions. This great divide formed a system in which the mutual projections interacted but did not correspond. It became a potentially enduring state of self-generating but self-defeating social demoralization (see below, Figs 12.2–12.4).

In this state, patients put on the spot by Nelly's crisp comments, and others in identification with them, felt the staff to be thrusting into the patients the anxieties which should really be for the staff to sort out. Thus, for example, references in the community meetings to the approaching leaving date were experienced by the patients not as useful insights, but instead as staff drawing attention to their own problems in such a way that it seemed then to make the patients responsible. The result of the patients' misperception was to generate a sullen resentment as if they had been accused of not being responsible enough; or alternatively they felt the responsibility was one they could not reject but which then seemed quite overwhelming. Whenever patients made tentative attempts to help, the staff, because of their different perceptions, did not react as if help was being offered. For the staff, that sort of assistance from patients felt as though further doubt was being cast on their own state, as though they were now being told by the patients as well, 'you can't be trusted to run this community, you have to be helped out'. So the staff response was then to put the problem back where they saw it as belonging – with the patients. They would then open the patients' eyes to their own faults and problems, such as poor attendance. Consequently, these patients were locked in a dilemma. In order to restore a sense of security they had to employ their more mature efforts, which, however, were then interpreted as their most neurotic. These kinds of staff-patient misperceptions were described above in chapter 8 on staff as the tranference object.

A total stalemate overtook the community. Any staff contribution was experienced by the patients as a denial of the staff disarray. The patients' best efforts were felt by the staff to be critical and potentially destructive.

It had been very unusual for this sort of state to last for as long as three months, but this time the solidity and self-reinforcing quality of the entrenched attitudes was very great. It was hard to see any way out of it, and the longer the stalemate continued, the more despair and demoralization mounted – and so the more intense the projection system became.

At the beginning of one week the demoralization was mentioned and forcefully placed in the context of the staff leaving and the need to re-form and regroup after they had gone. This coincided with making preparations for the programme for the monthly visitors day. It began to seem as though some possible re-forming of the community spirit began to take place around this event. The day after the visitors day there were congratulations from the staff on how well it had gone. The weather was very nice for the time of year. Spring was talked about, a new phase in the life of the community was anticipated by the staff who suddenly felt a relief and made it evident. The message must have seemed crystal clear to the patients – staff morale depended on the patients' spirit, their willingness and co-operation. The relief of the staff was such that it was experienced by the patients as a great burden of responsibility being thrown back on to them. Also, it suggested implicit blame for the very prolonged period in which things had been so unsatisfactory. A boisterous insistence by the staff that things would be different from now on encouraged a belief in the patients that the staff could not tolerate the demoralization any more, and they felt yet more pressure. This combination of burdensome responsibility, guilt and increased fear of the staff's weaknesses led the patients to retreat once again into an apathetic despair, tinged with a great deal of resentment at being imposed on in this way by the staff. They called the staff sergeant majors who drilled the patients into work groups. The general atmosphere had plunged into as bad a state as ever, such was the intractable nature of the community condition at the time.

How can a community turn this sort of corner? The very persistent nature of the division between staff and patients, and the almost total divorce between their separate attitudes and assumptions, made communications nearly impossible. The relatively sudden dissolving of this demoralized state came about in the course of two consecutive community meetings.

On a Thursday the meeting started with the difficulty of coming to grips with the absentee problem. A mood hanging over from the day before suggested that those who did not come must be unsuitable for a therapeutic community and should therefore be discharged. There was some unhappiness about this solution because it did seem to mean discharging rather a lot of people, and because it was felt that there must be some other means of approaching the problem. The idea was prevalent that the community ought to be able to help everyone that comes its way; also the feeling that if we cannot help everyone then we can help no-one. It was suggested in the meeting that those members who had been absent in the past but were present on that day could be questioned. And some were. They gave excuses about being ill, from flu, etc. The conversation tailed off when the excuses were not followed up or challenged. Next, Polly addressed Laura directly, saying that Laura had appeared to be upset about a particular matter the day before. The community had arranged a special lunch earlier in the week and Laura had taken some special responsibility for it. In fact the lunch had been a pleasant occasion except that only a very small proportion of the community had turned up. Some had gone off instead to eat elsewhere. Laura admitted her disappointment, that she felt hurt, and complained that anyone could have said they were not coming, but that she had organized for forty people and only a dozen came. Some people in the meeting were asked for their reasons for not coming to the lunch; and reasons such as the menu were given. A very hollow ring sounded in these excuses. It was pointed out that a previous event the week before had also been very poorly attended, although it had been very enjoyable for those who had taken part.

What was becoming clear was evidence of a further division in the community between those patients participating and taking responsibility and those uncommitted and absent. This was pointed out. After a brief recognition of this, and that there must be some shared attitudes and beliefs in the two sub-groups, the meeting turned back to another patient, Mary, who was sulky and pouring scorn and disfavour on all efforts to pay her attention and understand what her mood was about. Finally, she said she was going to leave. This seemed to crystallize the situation. Here was the uncommitted group actually going absent. It was now happening in dramatic form under our eyes. It became clear how severely it hit the community and injected further demoralization. The staff became angry and the patients silent and despairing. However, there was an achievement in that some open, shared recognition of the feelings of heavy responsibility and abandonment was made possible. This joint recognition between the staff and most of the patients led to new developments.

Something was happening on the patient side of the community. It is important to note this. The patients were dividing into two sub-groups. One can see that they correspond to the two different attitudes to the staff disarray: first, there were those who made efforts to be responsible but felt overburdened; second, there were those who felt persecuted and hence rejected the staff.

A new alignment was emerging, one which may have been latent previously but which now came to the fore visibly and could be distinguished from the dramatizations. The old formation of two sub-groups, patients and staff, was giving way to new sub-groupings. The patients were forming an active split around the responsibility problem. They can be referred to as patient group A for the committed ones, and patient group B for those like Mary who remained uninvolved. The feelings of being abandoned were shared between the staff and the committed group of patients (group A). It completely readjusted the dynamics, and the staff wasted no time in taking therapeutic advantage.

On the next day, Friday, these new sub-groupings began to form up. They clearly attracted a new projection system which put them into confrontation with each other. This meeting opened with Annie conveying a message from one of the absentees, Betty, who had not been to the hospital for about a week. We were told that she had probably discharged herself because she could not feel that the community was of use to her. There was then a good deal of discussion about what measures to take. At first people wanted to recommend that Betty should see a member of staff individually to discuss her future treatment, here or elsewhere. There was the assumption that there must be 'just the right place' for her. This optimism (or omnipotence) justified offering any possible alternatives that could be thought up. The community seemed to be falling into a typical posture of going on giving opportunities to someone who was kicking every one of them in the teeth. Yet at this point some members actually began to get angry. They objected that Betty should be allowed to get out of the normal routine of the community (she should come to the meeting to answer for her absence and to discuss her future with the community). The anger was therefore at her undermining the community and the efforts of those most responsible for keeping the community going. A long and heated discussion ensued – the first one for a very long time. The dispute ranged over the problem of catering for the individual versus maintaining the community organization.

Friday's community meeting, therefore carried on from the one the day before. It was trying to come to grips with the members who reject the meeting and why they do so. The lively discussion took place at the interface between the two patient sub-groups. It was enhanced by undistorted communications at last, between the staff and at least some of the patients (the more responsible ones). During the meeting, the guilt and persecution dissipated somewhat once it was realized that Betty could not expect tolerance and adaptation to her demands. The situation was relieved by honestly realizing that an ideal community did not exist. It was openly acknowledged that this group of people was easily hurt by rejection, and that Betty could not expect better than the reaction of a number of hurt people when she said she did not think they were of any use to her. This was a major realization. It cut through phantasies about an ideal community. The paranoid burden of guilt associated with the feeling of failure could be pushed towards a more realistic perspective.

The demoralization trap

The example reveals a number of patterns of interaction between the sub-groupings. To begin with, the low morale state is depressingly difficult to do anything about. This, in itself, aggravated the overall demoralization. Even when something went well – for example the visitors day – it went badly. There was no way out. This is a 'demoralization trap'. Once in, there seems to be no way out. Collectively, a community can begin a steady downward slide that no-one quite knows how to stop.

Furthermore, the spiral is mediated by a whole series of vicious circles of the kind described in the last chapter. There is no obvious point at which to intervene to stop the rot. The example is complex, with a number of interlocking cycles. At least five can be isolated. Their description, each with its corresponding diagram, will take up the rest of this chapter. Firstly, the staff have a problem amongst

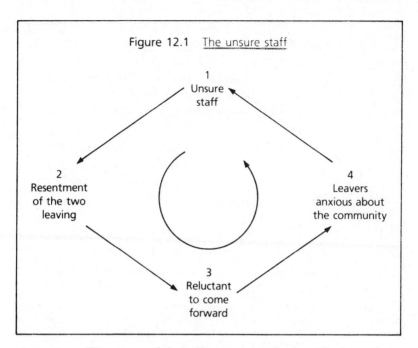

Figure 12.1   The unsure staff

themselves. The cause of their disarray went back to the loss of two members of the team. Figure 12.1 shows a cyclical train of consequences. The remaining staff felt unsure of themselves in the matter of taking over the community responsibilities (position 1). This led them to feel resentment towards those who were leaving (position 2) – and therefore they did not come forward to take over responsibilities before the leaving date (position 3). This made the two who were leaving anxious about the competence of those in whose hands they were leaving the community (position 4). Their anxiety about the remaining staff then fed back into the staff's self-doubt. The circle was complete.

The next two cycles deal with the two sub-groupings – the whole staff, and the patients. The staff felt unsure and criticized (position 1 in figure 12.2), and as a result of the crisis emotional difficulties were projected into the patient group (position 2) and dealt with energetically there. Staff dramatized this in 'therapizing' individual patients, putting them enthusiastically on the spot (position 3). This did not have the desired result. An ineffectual outcome of the therapizing was inevitable (position 4). The staff only felt less confident and more criticized, this time by the patients. The circle returned to position 1.

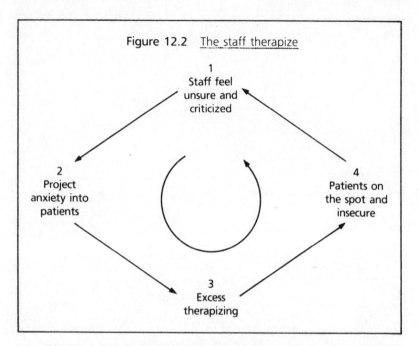

Figure 12.2   The staff therapize

Figure 12.3 describes a similar kind of cycle for the patient's side of the community. Patients felt insecure and abandoned (position 1) as a result of staff leaving, staff inadequacy, and lack of mutual support amongst themselves. They used the staff to project into, so that the staff's therapizing was experienced as anxiety and insecurity in the staff (position 2). The patients, or the majority of them, responded at first with support for and assistance to the staff (position 3). However, for the unsure staff this acted as confirmation of their inadequacy (position 4). This finally led back to the starting point with the patients feeling more insecure in the hands of the staff.

There is a correspondence between these last two circles, which may be summarized thus:

Position 1: primitive anxieties
Position 2: primitive defences
Position 3: dramatization
Position 4: outcome

In both instances (cycles) the dramatizations had poor outcomes. This is an inevitable consequence of the non-reality-based relationships

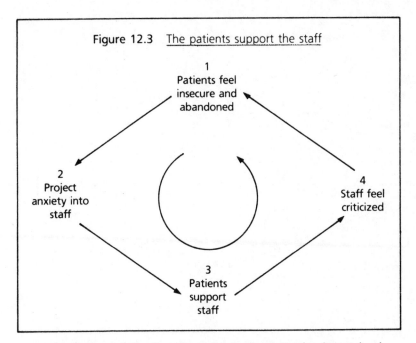

Figure 12.3   The patients support the staff

in dramatizations. It is clear from the figures how the dramatizations cause trouble. On the staff side, the therapizing fed into the primitive anxiety of the patients (feeling insecure and abandoned). The same was true of the other side – the dramatization of the patients ('the staff need support') fed into the staff's anxieties (feeling unsure and criticized).

These two interacting cycles can be combined in a single diagram (see Fig. 12.4). The notation refers to the positions in the staff (S) and patient (P) cycles in Figures 12.2 and 12.3 respectively.

The patient side of the community had two different sets of attitudes – I shall call the sub-groups P(a) and P(b). P(a) were those who reacted to the staff insecurity with guilt and a sense of omnipotent responsibility. P(b), the other sub-group, felt overburdened and resentful. These two sub-groups interacted with each other, forming another cycle which could be drawn to show how P(b)'s resentment and lack of attendance fed into the patient's sense of being abandoned – and also into the staff's feeling of being criticized.

Finally, as time went on P(b) became more significant, and quite suddenly a polarization between P(a) and P(b) mushroomed, and gathered in projections across the division which fundamentally

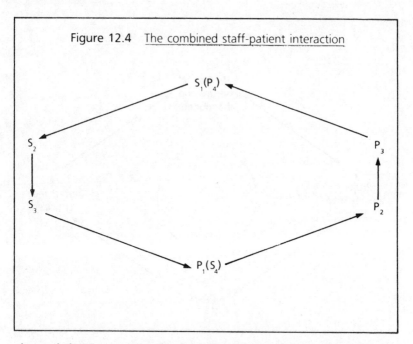

Figure 12.4 The combined staff-patient interaction

changed the community. Staff and P(a) linked up (position 1 in Fig.
12.5), and together they used P(b) into which to project irresponsibility. P(b) became the uncommitted (position 2). Staff and P(a)
combined, SP(a), established a solidarity. Now feeling secure they
managed to establish a more realistic view of the community. They
could assess their capacities and the possibilities of action. Perhaps
more important, they could begin to make a realistic assessment of
P(b). That is to say, they could assess the degree to which their
projections into P(b) conformed to the real characteristics of P(b).

   Coming to a realistic assessment of whom could be treated, and
working it out in relation to actual people (position 4) meant that the
illusion about omnipotence gave way. The efforts were not then bled
to death by a constant chasing after an elusive omnipotence which only
resulted in failures. As realistic attitudes towards the individuals
emerged (position 5), a protective attitude towards the community
developed. The price was to face the guilt and remorse (and anger)
about failing Betty (compare E 9.2, 'Facing the worst'). Eventually a
solution arose in which the community was able to say 'no' to Betty
(position 6). Previously she would have been the effective lead in a
dramatization of the weakness of the community, the criticism of the

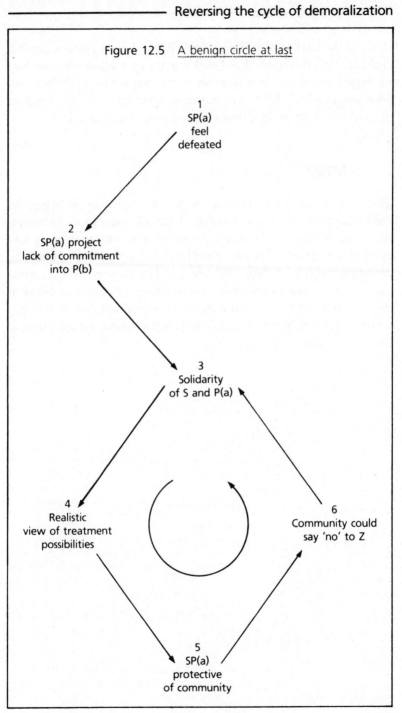

Figure 12.5 A benign circle at last

staff and the insecurity of the patients. When the community found it could say 'no', this strength fed back into the cycle again – but not into its beginning. It fed into position 3, starting a new cycle between positions 3 and 6. This turned out to be a benign circle. It started an upward spiral out of the demoralization trap at long last.

Summary

This chapter has been taken up with one illustration showing the difficulties of finding a way out of the demoralization spiral. As before, the cycles leading to the trapped state of demoralization were formalized in diagrams. The final emergence of a benign cycle pulled the community up again remarkably swiftly. The elements which turned the cycle into a benign one were a new and supportive alliance between the staff and some of the patients, and the confrontation of hitherto unmentionable problems such as who is really suitable for treatment in this community.

PART IV

The neurotic organization

13

Boundaries and barriers

Freud applied his discovery of the unconscious underlife of individuals to social phenomena (Freud, 1913; 1921). Jung was concerned with the idea of a collective unconscious (Jung, 1916). But the idea of collective defences has taken a long time to establish itself.

We have seen collective defences manifest themselves as dramatizations. They depend on processes of identification. The idea of collective defences based on identification processes was first elaborated by Jaques (1955). He extended the notion of transference to include the relationship of the individual to the social organization. The organization is conceived in phantasy terms by the individual member. But more than this, he showed in his pioneering work that groups of people develop shared attitudes and beliefs for the purpose of a psychological defence. In chapter 5 above, we saw Jaques' descriptions of the way individuals exploit the social milieu to externalize their own internal worlds (see above, pp. 70–1). The individuals collectively develop ideas about the character of their institution. These may be for defensive purposes, in which case they are based on unconscious phantasies. The collective view is a distorted form of the stated character and purpose of the institution. Jaques writes:

> *The form and content of institutions may thus be considered from two distinct levels; that of the manifest and consciously agreed form and content; and that of the phantasy form and content*

> *which are unconsciously avoided and denied, and, because they*
> *are totally unconscious, remain unidentified by members of the*
> *institution.* (1955, p. 497)

Jaques' idea was that one of the causes of groups of people remaining as groups is identification together on the basis of psychological defence. This would provide psychological gain for the individuals – albeit a restrictive gain. Although certain primitive anxieties (described in chapter 4, 'The internal community') are kept at bay, the price paid is the distortion of the institution, which is coloured by the splitting and projective and introjective identifications. The result is that the institution serves two masters – both the primary task and the psychological defence of the individuals which may express itself in a distortion of the task (which I termed task drift in chapter 9). When an organization functions in this second way, Jaques calls it a 'social defence system'.

A case study of a social defence system

Following Jaques' work, Menzies (1960) approached another institution as if it was a patient presenting a symptom. This was the nursing service of a London teaching hospital. The problem (symptom) that the organization presented was the alarming wastage of good student nurses. Menzies then set up a form of investigation starting with the 'symptom'. She established that the sources ran deep and appeared to involve very primitive anxieties and collectively operated defences. She noticed that nursing practice on the wards was organized in specific ways that were called 'good' nursing; yet these practices seemed to deny satisfaction to the nurses doing the job. In particular, the tasks were organized with other aims than the care of the patient. One was to distance the nurse as much as possible from any personal contact with the patient; and the other was to relieve the nurse of a sense of responsibility which was always passed up or down the hierarchy.

The personal distancing was accomplished by arranging the work in task lists – one nurse did all the bedpans, another all the temperatures. In this way the nurse did not relate to the whole person of the patient. This was reinforced by referring to patients by the number of the bed, or the disease, or the name of the diseased organ, etc.

These defensive 'techniques', as Menzies called them, were capped off by designating them 'good nursing' and by the assertion that a 'good' nurse does not get involved with her patient. This system was formally taught to the new student.

Menzies also showed that this was not just an arbitrary choice of the way to work. It acted as a defence and was determined by the impact of anxiety. The collective nature of the defence was particularly striking in this case study because there was a shared anxiety in the work itself. Barely adult new students were confronted by a task which involved very close proximity for a whole working shift with people who were in pain, mutilated or dying. It is in this sense that the practice is defensive. The personal distancing relieves the psychological endurance test presented to the vulnerable nurse.

The collective defences were of a very primitive kind. They avoided anxiety by projective and introjective defences, rather than facing it and working it through to achieve some maturation of the individual. Menzies writes: 'The social defence system represented the institutionalisation of very primitive defence mechanisms, a main characteristic of which is that they facilitate the evasion of anxiety, but contribute very little to its true modification and reduction' (Menzies, 1960). The upshot was that many of the individuals were actually more mature than the institution! For them, becoming a nurse meant an actual restriction of their own personality. Yet in order to continue her training, she was obliged to adopt the primitive defences of the institution – and for the more mature this was distressing. As a result it was often the better students who left!

The nurse was denied the job satisfaction of a natural personal contact with someone she helped; and also denied the opportunities for developing her own ways of confronting her own anxieties.

Do members of a therapeutic community institutionalize 'very primitive defence mechanisms, a main characteristic of which is that they facilitate the evasion of anxiety, but contribute little to its true modification and reduction'?

Is a dramatization a social defence system?

The dramatizations of a community meeting might be grasped as a symptom of the institution in a way similar to Menzies' approach.

Does a dramatization amount to a social defence system as discovered by Jaques and elaborated by Menzies?

I shall briefly enumerate the essential features of a social defence system for the purposes of comparison: (i) A social defence system is collective and gains advantage for the group of people involved because it provides the support of the group for each of the members; (ii) it is defensive because it protects the individuals from experiences that might be too unpleasant or overwhelming; (iii) the protection is effective against anxieties of a particularly threatening and primitive kind. These are the phantasy forms of anxiety that are harboured in the internal world; (iv) this use of the social system is an unconscious one. The form and content, however, will be rationalized as 'good' practices (as in the case about 'good nursing'); (v) the defensiveness depends especially upon primitive defences – splitting, and projective and introjective identification; (vi) because of social pressure to adopt an identity or role, the system leads to a restriction of the personality; (vii) as well as the problem it brings to the individual personality, the social defence system leads to an equally rigid institution which defeats its own purpose and is extremely difficult to change.

Dramatizations do in fact have these same characteristics: (i) they are collective (see E 5.3, 'A collective projection'); (ii) they are defensive; (iii) they are defensive against the internal anxieties of the individuals (see E 4.2, 'A mother's remorse'); (iv) they cause people to be trapped in them without conscious awareness of participating (see E 1.1, 'The meeting that went wrong'); (v) these roles represent the operation of primitive defence mechanisms – *splitting* (see, for example, E 5.1, 'Splitting off a role'), *projective identification* (see, for example, E 6.2, 'The disowned identity'), and *introjective identification* (see, for example, E 6.1, 'The man who thought he wanted to be himself', E 6.3, 'The monologuist', E 6.4, 'The silent member'); (vi) the individual is often restricted to the role in an anti-therapeutic way (see, for example, E 4.1, 'The persecuted victim'); and (vii) the institution suffers through a distortion of the task (as discussed in chapter 9).

As it manifests itself in the community meeting, dramatization is clearly a form of social defence system. Menzies' nursing service would appear to have institutionalized the dramatization of an object-relationship of no emotional contact – a non-feeling, numbed, mechanical caring. This external drama replicates an internal world of despair and phantasy of irredeemable damage to others.

The nursing staff were in fact only one side of the social structure. Menzies says very little about the patients and their social system. However, through contiguity with the culture carriers – the nurses – their role was to be the anonymous bearers of an ill organ, remaining passive in bed, without emotion, motion or individual identity. Such a role of passive inertia may be interpreted by the patient in his own way, but often collective sets of attitudes may emerge through introjective processes.

They may idealize the staff, and the work of nursing, to defend against anxieties about their own illnesses and mortality. Thus the staff become filled with a great potency. If they appear to remain remote, the patients may rationalize this as due to the specially intense demand for such specially competent staff.

There is no point in speculating further about the patients' collective defences. However, the point has been made in the example in the last chapter (see E 12.1, 'Rescuing morale') that in a stable system there is a 'fit' between the various sub-groupings. In that example the demoralization arose from the cyclical intertwining of staff and patient attitudes. A dramatization means a system in which the members of a sub-group not only introject attitudes from each other to form the group identification, but also introject from the adjacent sub-group in a way that confirms their own group identification.

Barrier-formation

Jaques was particularly aware of this state of unarticulated interlocking of the structure. In his own study of the social defence system of a factory he showed that the sub-groups interacted but did not properly communicate. His descriptions showed very clearly how attempts at discussion and joint decision-making between management and the workforce were frustrated by suspicions, hostility and guilt on both sides, coming from quite unrealistic attitudes towards each other (Jaques 1951).

One of the ways in which he summarized his findings was in terms of the communication processes within the organization. When both sub-groups projected into each other, this affected the communications between them. A mutual projection system of this kind will be described below, in E 14.5, 'The day community penetrated'.

Jaques recognized that the organization was split up into sub-groups for a functional division of labour. Communication between these sub-groups tended to be restricted. For instance, colleagues working together in the same workshop talked more to each other than to colleagues in different workshops. He called this an adaptive segregation, although we may as well retain the simple term 'boundary'.

However, the organization is also split apart by phantasy based on the primitive defences. Communications are then restricted in a different way. They are affected by hostility, suspicion and guilt, and this leads to persistent misperceptions of the other group, and of their communications and intentions. Communication is seriously distorted or blocked by this emotional filtering. Jaques calls this maladaptive segmentation – but the simpler term 'barrier' is quite sufficient here.

Ordinary boundaries in the organization may become twisted into barriers. Barriers may also arise where there is no normal structural boundary (this will be studied in detail in chapter 14). The following example is taken from David Cooper's account (1967, pp. 111-12) of his unit in a large mental hospital

E 13.1 Phantastical communication

'Nowhere were anxieties more evident than in the highly significant distortions of the hospital communication process. Reports are submitted to the nursing office by the nurse in charge of the unit at the end of each shift. Sometimes these reports travel via the night nursing superintendent to the day shift of nursing administrators. At each change of hands the reports are edited, "significant" happenings in each ward being selected for presentation in a final version of the daily meeting of doctors, social workers, and nursing officers on the division. A typical incident processed by this communication system was the following: a young man in the unit had a girl-friend in a female ward; one night she became hysterically upset about an issue connected with her ward and treatment, and he and a friend attempted to console her and help her back to her ward; she noisily resisted these attempts and a member of the portering staff who witnessed the incident called a nurse who took her back to the ward. The porter informed the night nursing superintendent, who informed the unit and reported to the day nursing administration, who reported finally to the divisional meeting. The final version was that two male patients from the unit had attacked a female patient and, it was implied, were attempting to carry her off for sexual purposes. The phantasy existing in the minds of many staff outside the unit is that rape, sexual orgies, and murder are daily occurrences in the unit.'

The grit in the cogwheels

The idea that an organization can be infiltrated by psychologically determined disruptions is an important one. Because it is an unconscious process, these features are impervious to conscious efforts to change the system. We could think of 'a neurotic organization'. However, the grit that gets in between the cogwheels of the organization is still the pain and the defensiveness of the individuals. Main has given a vivid account of this interface between the organization and the individual. He gave examples from his experience in wartime and observed that two units in the army may have quite different levels of morale and of expressed psychological disturbances. The structure of the two units is inescapably the same – it is laid down in the army handbook. However, some units carry a lot of members with individual neurotic disturbance, whilst others throw up much absenteeism, illness, breakdown and other indices of pathology. He concluded that each unit had its own system for operating the given structure. And that it depended on the individuals involved. The crucial point was that something got into the structure, something more important but more hidden, 'the human folkways by which the structure is operated' (Main, 1977). This contrast between the formal structure and the individual human folkways corresponds to Jaques' manifest form and content contrasted with the unconscious phantasy form and content.

Group structure and personality structure

This view of boundaries and their vicissitudes derives from the background of Kleinian theory developed in Britain, and I have

163

applied it with psychoanalytic intentions to a therapeutic task. In Rice's work he has taken much the same theoretical base, but developed it in the service of consultancies to organizations of 'normal' people. In his development he has embraced systems theory, and the importance of the boundaries of the various systems (individual and organizational).

In contrast to my approach is that based on ego-psychology, and in particular the theory of primary boundlessness described by Mahler (1975) before the psychological birth of the infant. These views have been applied to groups (Klein, 1981; Oskarsson and Klein, 1982; Greene, 1982; Kernberg, 1984). In these approaches boundaries are important since they represent the adequacy, or otherwise, of the ego in one of its prime functions, to maintain its separateness and to prevent a slipping back into the primary fusion. Thus boundaries of the group are to be sustained, by the group leader or the staff team, *on behalf of* the weak egos of the group members (see Greene and Johnson, 1987; Klein and Brown 1987) – witness, for instance, 'the need for a clear, strong, palpable and relatively indestructible social system' (Swenson, 1986, p. 161).

This application of the ego-psychology model is quite different to the one presented here, based on Kleinian theory – which rests on the view (opposed to Mahler) that object-relations exist from birth and that there is therefore a primary boundary between self and others from the outset. As a result, boundary problems are viewed as expressions of the internal problems. Thus in the one view there is an emphasis on the ego's capacity for boundary maintenance, and in the present view an emphasis on the structure of the ego (its internal boundaries). The vicissitudes of boundaries are thus seen as features of group life to be controlled, in the ego-psychology view; whereas in my view they are features of group life to be analysed. The vicissitudes of the boundaries are not merely to be attributed to weak egos collected together under one roof, but are to be examined, to show how and why a difference becomes an opposition, a separation becomes a rigid split and so on.

In my view, whatever action one has to take in groups – which certainly may get out of order, especially in a therapeutic community setting – it is best to understand first how the problem has arisen out of the projective systems that create the social defence system.

In the next chapters I wish to follow up the idea of the disordered community organization and show its various forms. I shall exploit Jaques' concept of the barrier distorting communication, in order to explore a whole range of community phenomena. Much of this will relate to the problems of a loss of integrity and fragmentation. Barriers do indeed lead to splitting of the organization and to the threat of its fragmentation.

Summary

This chapter has introduced certain concepts used in describing and understanding features of an organization interfered with by the personal distress of the members. The possibility of the whole system being distorted into a socially operated defence has been described independently by Jaques and Menzies. The dramatizations described in this book resemble and confirm the discovery of social defence systems. The notion of a communication barrier formed by emotional states deriving from the use of projection and introjection between groups is important. The relations between groups can be investigated in the same way as the dramatized relations between individuals. The concepts of boundary and barriers, derived from Jaques, are helpful in understanding the inter-group phenomena explored in the following chapters.

14

The caprice of the barrier

The processes described in the earlier chapters are flickering patterns that come and go largely in the undifferentiated medium of the large community meeting. We will now investigate the community organization as whole.

Taking a step back from the community meeting, what comes into view is a system of staff and patients. This whole system is alive on all planes – material, sensual, political, social and organizational – a well-rounded, fully-developed organism that is not homogeneous. It is fully differentiated with its own organizational and functional structure. If in the community meeting it was usually individuals playing out relationships, in the whole community it is the different parts of the structure. In a multi-group system, the inter-group relations are as significant as the inter-personal.

Any group that lasts for more than a brief period of time develops the collective idea that it is good to be a member of the group. The identity of the group comes to be established through such collective attitudes and they are often carried one step further to the point of view that it is not so good to be a member of some other group (specified or unspecified). Further development of the collective idea can even assert that because the group exists, therefore it has a useful or beneficial function. A later example illustrates this (see E 16.2, 'The ossified meeting'). The group's purpose may remain unspecified; and the point is that the value of the group and its purpose is self-evident without mention or question. Shenker (1986) makes the point that the ideology of a group or community has the function of ensuring that membership of the community is valued highly and will keep the member embedded within it. Internal beliefs within the group about its value and its nature are closely linked to and affected by relationships with other external groups. For instance, a rapid method for uniting a group is to discover a common enemy.

Manning (1976) has shown the way in which different apsects of the programme acquire different values, and that this changes from time to time, and also from place to place. This is confirmed by many other observers, for instance McKeganey (1986), Stockwell, Powell and Bhat (1986), and by many of the examples in this book (for example, E 14.7, 'The special group of students', and E 14.8, 'The emotional hot potato'). In this chapter we will examine this in terms of the boundaries and barriers between groups in this 'multi-group' system. The way in which an individual identifies with and 'belongs' to a part of the organization is under the influence of other groups which may be open or closed to him. Equally, the ways in which he values himself and the group go hand in hand.

The barrier moves around the structure

Traditional mental hospitals are, or were, characterized by an extraordinarily stable barrier lying between the patients and the staff. I use the term barrier as defined in the previous chapter, and it will be illustrated in the following example. The implication is that the organization operates as a social defence system. In Fig. 14.1, 'The hospital multi-group system', the structural position of this staff/patient barrier is indicated. Actually, barriers could be placed in various sites, and this will be studied below (see Fig. 14.3). The traditional staff/patient barrier of the mental hospital has been exhaustively described by Goffman (1961), Kesey (1962) and many others. There is no choice about which group to belong to and each side views the other with characteristic suspicion, fear, pity and guilt. This is a boundary which has become a barrier and has taken permanent root – has become institutionalized. Rosenberg (1970) has shown it to be defensive in exactly the same way as the system studied by Menzies.

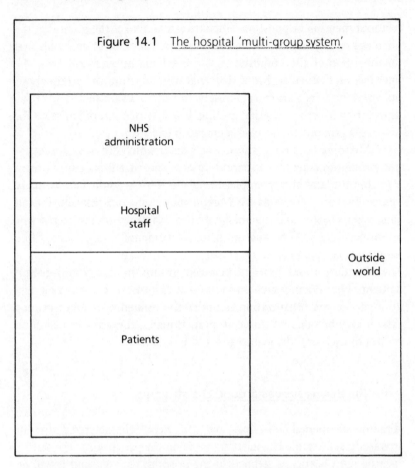

Figure 14.1   The hospital 'multi-group system'

The origins of the therapeutic community lay in the attempt to remove this barrier between patients and staff. The intention was to reveal a new life in the institution which would bring out the potential left in the patients rather than stripping them further to a state of anonymous ineptitude. However, very often the barrier was not removed but merely moved. Cooper showed this vividly, (see E 13.1, 'Phantastical communication', and it is illustrated again in the following example).

E 14.1 **The TC ward**

David Clark relates the story of therapeutic community principles being introduced into a ward embedded in the entrenched, stereotyped patterns of an old style mental hospital (Clark, 1964). The doctor, he says, 'approached the medical superintendent who had expressed general interest in these ideas and asked permission to run the ward as a therapeutic community. He had talks with the matron, the ward sister, the nursing tutor, and each of the senior psychiatrists about what he hoped to do.

'He reorganised the ward around community meetings, small group meetings, and frequent staff discussions. The experiment went well. The patients stopped grumbling about the food and began to talk about their feelings about one another and the staff, their fears and anxieties, and began openly to face their desire for dependence and fears of discharge. The staff began to discuss their own dissensions and disagreements, to criticise one another, and to modify some of the professional rigidities. The ward became a much livelier though untidier place; the staff and patients on the ward, with some hesitations, welcomed the changes.'

The old barriers to communication were coming down, stereotypes were dissolving. It all seemed straightforward after so many decades of the traditional system. David Clark was happier. But wait a minute – 'The repercussions from the rest of the hospital were sharp. His fellows amongst the junior doctors criticised the disorder and the fact that they were called down at night about rows between patients. They also pointed out to him that he was wasting his time with this stuff when he might be pursuing his career. Other senior nurses were very critical of the ward sister. Rumours ran round the hospital that the place encouraged unethical medical practices among the nurses. Patients on other wards were unwilling to be transferred to the unit.'

The complaints of the senior nurses suggest that the service may have developed similar practices to the one studied by Menzies and that there was an objection to dissolving that defensiveness. The change in the barrier is illustrated in figure 14.2. Instead of a barrier between staff and patients, there arose a new barrier between those inside the ward (staff plus patients) and those outside (patients as well as staff), very reminiscent of E 13.1, above, 'Phantastical communication'.

The next example again demonstrates a shifting barrier. It alights in several places which can be followed with the help of a further diagram (see Fig. 14.3).

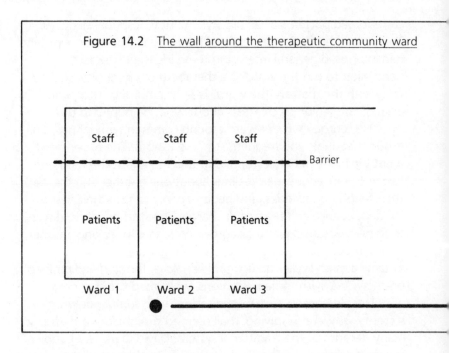

Figure 14.2   The wall around the therapeutic community ward

E 14.2 **The mobile barrier**

There was a severe crisis in the relations between the
community and the administrative authority of the National
Health Service at the time. There was a clash over the whole
future and survival of the hospital. The community did survive,
and in spite of quite profound feelings of suspicious mistrust,
relatively good relations were eventually re-established
(Grunberg, 1973). It was noticeable that following this period of
crisis and the identification of a serious external enemy, a
striking and highly unrealistic perception developed. The
community and the outside world were polarized. This was no
longer a case of a barrier between the community and the
administration (see Fig. 14.3 (b)). It had moved on to position
(c) in figure 14.3. The community thought of itself as a haven
(see E 5.4, 'The community as paradise', from this same period).
Both patients and staff held this exaggerated view. This became
clear in various ways: patients expected unnecessarily long

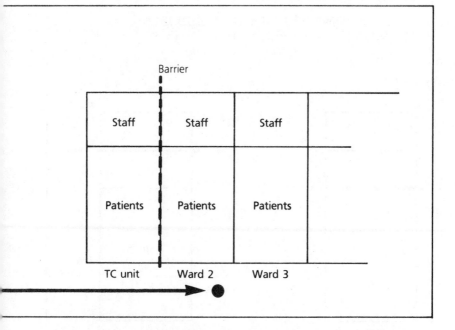

stays; there was a reluctance to participate in the programme for outside visitors; and the existence of unpleasant incidents was denied. One incident was referred to in E 5.4: Don dangerously hurled a piece of wood across the workshop during a period when his discharge was being negotiated. The following day the community meeting avoided this incident, which had frightened those present. Instead the meeting concentrated on how alien the outside world was. Landlords and bosses were contrasted with the comfort and indulgence inside the community. This collective blindspot indicated a seriously distorting barrier. The meeting itself had a general sense of warmth and comfort to it. Because this was accepted as a fact, the staff began to think that it promoted dependence, and that in the interests of the patients the community should be less indulgent and make sterner demands on the patients. As a direct result of that meeting the staff resolved to institute a tougher programme. When the staff pursued this, the barrier moved again. The staff developed distorted views about the patients – they saw them as comfortable rather than desperate. The structure now resembled Figure 14.3 (a), with a barrier between the patients and the staff.

171

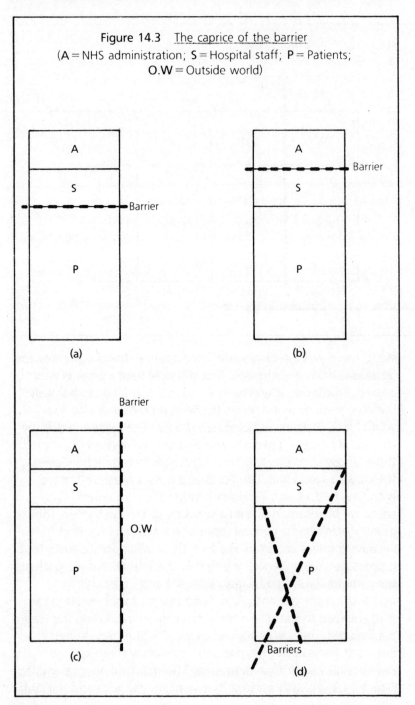

Figure 14.3   The caprice of the barrier
(A = NHS administration; S = Hospital staff; P = Patients;
O.W = Outside world)

Because the staff's views and actions were based on the projection system gathering around the staff/patient boundary, their efforts ran aground. Patients merely projected the unpleasant demands outside the hospital even more strongly.

A further movement took place (described in more detail in example 18.1 below, 'Tackling the attendance problem'). A sub-group of patients began to be identified who were supposed to represent the people who used the community and the hospital in a particularly dependent way but who remained unhelped. They were often very poor attenders and were regarded as therefore irresponsible and intractibly disturbed. Perhaps some of them were, but they came to represent it for the staff and for the other patients in a particularly black and white way. A new projection system was developing. This 'diagonal' split is illustrated in Figure 14.3 (d), with a new barrier between the staff plus some patients on one side and the rest on the other side.

The point of this example is to show the mobility of the barrier in a multi-group system that is set up to avoid the institutionalization of the old mental hospital system. The following table summarizes these dynamic shifts.

Stage	Barrier position between two sub-groups	Schema in Fig. 14.3
1	community/administration	b
2	community/outside world	c
3	patients/staff	a
4	good attenders/poor attenders	d

In the rest of this chapter we will consider various aspects of this barrier formation within a multi-group system.

The inter-group arena

The next example comes not from the community but from a report of a conference set up to study these dynamics. The report describes the

impact of inter-group relations on the effectiveness of three groups
formed in a special 'inter-group exercise' (Higgin and Bridger, 1965,
p.29).

E 14.3 **The group carrying guilt**

The exercise started with an invitation to the total membership of
the event to form three groups, and the response was an
immediate and shattering flight from the large group. It was
described as a 'dramatic explosion in the first few seconds of the
Exercise'. The report continues: 'The guilt and the aggression that
was left behind at the outset had to be dealt with by the
conference in its various groups if it were to get on with its task.
The conference also had to contain the continuing temptation to
flight, throughout the task. It did this by creating in Z group a
part of itself that carried the emotional burden for the whole. Z
continued in flight from the task. It remained disturbed and
unable to work because of its pre-occupation with the guilt that
had arisen from the first flight, which it had absorbed on behalf
of the whole conference ... Because of the special emotion-
containing role the group was carrying it was not free to take
decisions for itself or to contribute to those of the whole ...
Because Z group was doing this job and having these elements in
X and Y groups projected into it and, in turn, introjecting them, it
was possible for the other two groups to be sufficiently free from
this basic assumption to get on with the task.'
　　The point being made is that one of the groups retained the
primitive response of fleeing from facing the problem, so that the
other groups could attain to a less primitive mode of operating.
The authors go on: 'In this way, all the groups can be seen to
have accepted, and in their different ways acted on, the task ...
Thus it can be said that all three groups took an equal share of
the work of the conference as a whole, of which they were all
part.'

It is important to recognize these processes, partly because they have a
very potent influence on the apparent effectiveness of the groups, and
partly because in groups in a therapeutic community the task must be

to trace the movements of guilt, aggression and anxiety. This is at least as important as getting a group to go well! This point will be emphasized in the course of further examples.

A group that seems to go better than others cannot be strictly compared in such terms. The 'good' group may depend on the badness of the 'bad' group. One might become suspicious of a defensive management of experience when sub-groups begin to perceive the difference between them in terms of 'good' and 'bad'. The next example demonstrates the way in which guilt is pushed around the system, so that it is always in 'the other'.

E 14.4 The in-group and the out-group

In discussions following a phase of serious and dangerous acting out, it became apparent that members viewed the community as having two classes – an in-group who dominated meetings verbally and an out-group who did not, and who by implication had to act out. One particular patient was a fire-setter who, until this division had been noted, was mute in the community meetings. During ensuing discussions there was a good deal of guilt around. Those in the in-group blamed the members of the out-group for not talking in the meetings and for not expressing verbally what they had been acting out. The out-group, by acting out, were putting the in-group in the wrong for dominating.

One could say that the in-group were apparently functioning very well, were using the groups – that is to say, were talking in them. However, bearing in mind Higgin and Bridger's views, did the out-group in fact resemble their Z group? Did the out-group carry an emotional experience for the whole? It seems very likely that it did. The out-group carried the experience of being left out in the cold (hence a 'need' to set a fire). This was projected by the in-group; and in turn introjected by the out-group. The in-group also projected guilt which in fact the out-group did not introject. Instead, they immediately re-projected it in order to establish that the dominating in-group was to blame.

The group which appears to be working well may get its come-uppance. The next example shows how a 'star' department in the hospital was particulary vulnerable to disruption.

E 14.5 **The day community penetrated**

For a period of three years or so previously, a conscious attempt
had been made to develop the day community along the lines of
a therapeutic community proper. To do this eventually entailed a
functional split within the adult department of the hospital. The
intention was to create a boundary as defined in the last chapter,
to separate two groups of staff. The day community staff formed
a sub-group of their own consisting of those who were more
involved with day patients and who were on the whole full-time.
As this developed the staff most involved formed closer and more
satisfying relationships (both amongst themselves and with their
patients). The day community adopted the banner of the
therapeutic community and took on something of a star role in
the hospital. Community meetings and staff meetings had
previously been open to any of the adult department staff, and
this had caused difficulty in running the community. Decision-
making was slow, and at times ill-informed. Manipulation of one
staff member against another had been common, and chronicity
amongst the patients was an endemic problem. These various
problems had been attributed to the difficulty in keeping
everyone up to date on events as they happened – especially the
part-time staff who, like some of the patients, were irregular or
occasional attenders at meetings. The solution chosen was
intended to keep the part-time staff separate and out of day
community matters, and to give them charge of out-patients.
This solution was imposed unilaterally by the day community
staff, and included asking the part-time staff not to attend
meetings. The unilateral nature of the decision was important.
  The solution worked well in terms of communication and
efficiency, but only so long as the boundary was kept intact
between the day community staff and the rest. However, a
dynamic reminiscent of Higgin and Bridger's example was thrown
up. The 'rest', who were to become the out-patient department,
felt that they had been pushed out – felt themselves to be also-
rans, second-rate, exiles. This in-or-out dynamic resembles the last
example, and it was felt painfully by the out-patient staff.
However, the day community staff were given a boost and
morale soared. Yet it was at the expense of the out-patient staff.

The state of the out-patient staff was unorganized, demoralized and lacking cohesion, identity or policy. The morale problems of the day community staff were pushed into a newly created part of the organization – the out-patient department.

Norman was a new senior member of staff appointed to take over responsibility for the out-patient department and to be the focus around which this ragged group could form and develop. But imagine the impact on this poor new appointee faced not only with establishing himself but also with creating a new department with material which had the stigma of left-overs! Initially his interest in the day community was slight, but showed a marked increase within two or three months. Norman began to come regularly to certain of the day staff meetings, the reason being to allow him to become familiar with the work of the day community. However, a curious thing began to happen. He started to present to the day community staff a particular clinical problem that kept cropping up in the out-patient department. He brought the case up regularly – and no matter how often it was discussed, no progress was made. The case concerned an ex-patient of the day community who had been discharged in a more or less unchanged condition. He could be regarded as a failure of the day community, and had somehow slid over to one of the out-patient staff for some unspecified support. Ostensibly, the case was brought up to define the boundary between day community work and that of the out-patient department. Norman would at the same time both assert the existence of his new department and complain that it was not in a position to take over ex-day patients (as indeed it should not). However, the repetitiveness and the lack of progress indicated mysterious forces at work. On occasions the business of these meetings was hampered for long periods. In spite of proclaiming the separateness of the out-patient department, Norman was acting out a real interference of one in the other.

The case which was so persistently brought back to the day staff was one of their own throw-outs. That is to say, the patient was an apt representation of what the out-patient staff felt themselves to be.

The day community had achieved its 'star' quality by literally splitting off its dejection and inefficiency and projecting them very concretely into the out-patient department in the form of rejected colleagues. The emotional experience was then brought back to the day staff once more when the out-patient department managed to establish its own self-respect. However, it was brought back in a special form – it was called a patient. For the day community staff, it represented the ineffectiveness and failure which they had wanted to rid from their experience. For the out-patient staff, it represented the experience of being thrown out which they wanted to get rid of. It would have been important to realize that in the repetitive discussions we were not dealing with a case, but negotiating how to deal with a fragment of experience.

The work of both departments had to be carried on, not just at the level of administrative and professional efficiency, but also at the level of the emotional identity of the group.

E 14.6 Exiles in a group

During this period when the out-patient department were forming themselves into an organized section of the hospital, they decided to set aside one of their own staff meetings for other members of the hospital staff to attend as visitors in order to see the work of the new department. This invitation was taken up by a number of people. A discussion on out-patient group psychotherapy was planned. However, the discussion took a strange and obsessive turn, becoming bogged down in one particular tangential issue – whether or not it was advisable to include foreigners in out-patient groups. The relevance of this was lost on the visitors.

The out-patient staff was engaged in a selective activity which reflected their own task of forming a cohesive group out of exiles. They had to cope with the emotional work of feeling like refugees themselves, pushed out of 'home' and dumped together as a group. Although talked about as patients, foreigners really represented the problem that the out-patient staff had in treating their own feeling of being exiles.

The functioning of the two staff groups was intertwined for some time after the original split which had triggered off the polarized feelings of exclusiveness and exile. It was present at least fifteen months later. Interestingly, Norman – who was most active in carrying the projection back – was not even on the staff at the time of the split.

The group which goes well

Groups which appear to work well and groups which appear to go badly should not be taken at face value. They take on 'an equal share of the work'. In the next example a special three-month programme was all but sabotaged and sunk by similar undiagnosed inter-group dynamics.

E 14.7 The special group of students

During the summer vacation period six university students were admitted as day patients for a three-month programme (Hinshelwood and Foster, 1978). This was a considerably shorter stay than the average patient. The group was therefore rather separate and different – a characteristic that was enhanced by all being admitted together. In the first two months the separateness made for a feeling of being rather special, a feeling that was again enhanced by the experimental nature of the whole project.

A crisis point was reached, however, at the beginning of their third month. There were various factors that came together. First, one of the co-therapists in the small group for these students went on holiday, and on one occasion the small group had to meet on its own because the other therapist was away for two days. At the same time, the middle month of the scheme was used to make personal reviews of each of the six people in the scheme and their own progress so far. This had marked quite clearly the passing of the half-way point. Finally, one member of the group was offered individual sessions outside the group in conjunction with her boyfriend. These were factors leading to the crisis in which the sense of being special flipped over and delivered a resounding backlash.

At first there were arguments and rows as demoralization set in. Then, for one meeting (the first for which the co-therapist was away), everything suddenly seemed to come together in a desperate flight into health. Thereafter things went from bad to worse. The next group session was dominated by disaffection with the remaining therapist. There were more arguments and open talk of the group going to pieces. One person announced he had himself made arrangements to go on holiday for two weeks. A day later, a second member decided to drop out and went home. A week later a third got a job and left. The group had lost half of its membership. The rest were demoralized. They suddenly took more part in the other aspects of the community, attending the community meetings with a greater degree of involvement.

This shows a desperate attempt to find an alternative security when the small group was flying apart. The initial high morale rested on a major projection of despair into the rest of the community which protected a spurious feeling of being special. This was a precarious basis for morale. When the crisis hit, the resources for holding the group together were inadequate. First, there was a flight from the experience into a pseudo-unity for one session, which itself quickly moved into an actual fragmentation – amplifying the demoralization in a now familiar vicious circle.

It is clear that the 'good' performance of the group is only apparent. In the first two months there was something unrealistic about the group, since the members relied on being special. The initial success and confidence were quickly removed when the specialness wore thin. There had not been a full recognition of the despair, nor of the projective method of dealing with it. It was nearly too late before there came a realization of the most important collective opportunity for working with the despair. There is more to tell about this inter-group projection.

E 14.8 The emotional hot potato

The therapist who was responsible for the small group work of this summer vacation scheme was, as it happens, one of the usual small group therapists in the day community who had her own group of ordinary day patients as well. During this summer period she was therefore therapist of two small groups in the community – group S (students) and group D (ordinary day patients). As we have seen, the students' arrival created a special group in the community. It was D group more than any other group in the community that was affected. And D group particularly introjected the despair – carrying it for S group and the rest of the community. It happened that at this time D group was itself in a fragile state. There were in fact several members who, being characteristic 'actors-out', were enacting the demoralization through erratic attendance. The effect of the rather special group S was to drive D group further into the doldrums, and the group all but ceased to exist. Attendance became even more erratic, there was little attempt to work and mutism appeared. It seemed to D group that, compared with S group, they must be totally uninteresting to their therapist and they had nothing worth saying. It was proved by the attention the therapist was turning on to the special newcomers. This might be sibling rivalry, but at the group and inter-group level it was much more pernicious and difficult to handle when acted out in non-attendance.

Finally, there was a remarkable turn-around in D group, just at the moment when S group hit its crisis. D group bucked up and found new heart, attendance improved and the efforts to work revealed more energy. The demoralization passed from D group to S group literally like a hot potato.

The polarization between two groups connected by the same therapist actually changed their character, through the impact of each upon each other. The initial high morale of S group was fed by their awareness of a rival group that was deeply demoralized. In turn, the low morale of D group fed on the awareness of these special intruders. Yet things could change abruptly when the projection system broke down.

The fate of S group is important. The example shows it starkly. For the students, the chance of therapy was limited enough because of the length of their vacation, and it was seriously jeopardized by having a proper phase of termination aborted.

The magic mountain

Thomas Mann's novel was of a tuberculosis sanitorium which had become a retreat, remote and cut off from life outside. The novel *The Magic Mountain* has given its name to a phenomenon observable frequently in the therapeutic community (see van den Langenberg and de Natris, 1985). The neglect of the outside world has psychodynamic roots. The motivation to draw attention away from the outside world and on to the internal group processes of the therapeutic community is sometimes an important occurrence in groups and in the therapeutic community. Although barely recognized in small therapeutic groups, it is particularly apparent in the therapeutic community since this cutting off from the demands of the real world poses risks to the survival of the community.

In this case the world outside the therapeutic community is attributed with certain noxious or threatening characteristics which the community then avoids. This is quite common and can be seen in various of the examples in this book (see E 5.4, 'The community as paradise' and E 14.1, 'The TC ward' in this chapter; also E 18.1, 'Tackling the attendance problem'). McKeganey (1986) also describes an interesting comparison between two communities in roughly the same organizational environment, but with different attitudes to it. One of them has clearly curled up into an oblivious fascination with its own internal processes, and is unhappily in danger on the magic mountain.

The magic mountain syndrome is a case in which the task of the community is so assiduously followed that it becomes maladaptive, and results from the creation of a barrier around the community rather than a flexible and semi-permeable boundary. We have seen that this kind of perversion of the task of the community is very common (for example, E 9.1, 'Therapizing the individual'). Schlunke and Garnett (1986) give a recent case in point; and Baron (1987) describes in detail a striking example of the maladaptive withdrawal into the community, which neglected all demands from outside.

The survival of the community is in jeopardy if the boundary around the community, and its task in the real world outside the community, is seriously affected by the development of a barrier which becomes the site of a defensive projection system. It is equally true that the projections the external world make into the therapeutic community are also important. Bott (1976) discusses this in relation to the mental hospital as a whole, and she shows how the importation of madness puts the hospital staff into a stress and a particular form of three-way conflict that comes from contradictory social attitudes outside the hospital. Mendizabal (1985) describes the effect on a community of a national economic crisis.

The magic mountain syndrome is a problem of the boundary around the community as a whole. Disorder to this boundary has particularly damaging effects on the capacity to work realistically in the wider environment. Having issued this caution, in the next chapter we will begin to look in a more systematic way at the kinds of groups and communities that exist.

Summary

This chapter has gathered together a number of illustrations of the dramatizations which occur between groups. One feature of these is the barrier to communication between the groups which are caught up in a mutual projection system. These distorted group identities, based on primitive projection and introjection, take the form of a very concrete transfer of feelings and experiences between groups. They are often transferred in the form of a patient.

15

Disruption and fragility

The examples at the end of the last chapter, E 14.7 ('The special group of students') and E 14.8 ('The emotional hot potato'), showed the many complex factors involved in the fragile state of two groups which very nearly came to the point of total fragmentation.

The community, too, can be fragile. It has, through introjection, a very potent meaning for the members (see chapter 4 on the internal community). The evidence suggests that fear is one of the most important influences in group cohesion. The crippled organization has many aspects, which we will look at in this and subsequent chapters.

Interference by an individual

I shall start with the way in which the internal world of the individual can create havoc with the cohesion of the community.

E 15.1 The quarrelsome intruder

Ben, a patient, was present at the community meeting in which a number of people were arranging to set up an accommodation committee to try to find homes, a persistent problem for day patients in London. Ben owned his own house and was not in difficulties in this respect. He could not join the committee as a needy member. However, he made a point of taking part in the discussion in the meeting. And he did so in a characteristic way. He fastened on to a particular point: Charlie had suggested that the Church Commissioners might offer a house for rent. Ben took Charlie to task about how to make this kind of approach. He advocated caution and an approach through personal contacts. In the manner of his speech, he appeared to be accusing Charlie of incaution. There ensued ten minutes of unfriendly and domineering exchange over this detail, which prevented the meeting from getting on with its efforts to form a committee.

On another occasion the community was discussing arrangements for a jumble sale. Up to that point Ben had not been involved in any of the work. Now he realized that he was not part of the community activity. In exactly the same way as before he appeared to have the interests of the jumble sale at heart, but in the manner of his speech he appeared accusatory and provoked bickering. Once again, discussion of the arrangements was held up.

Ben's typical relationship with the community work was a pseudo-involvement to cope with his own feelings of being left out of some satisfactory work in progress. He was a middle-aged man with a dour and puritanical attitude to life who, in spite of his querulous and paranoid disposition, had been not unsuccessful. He was a hard-working self-sufficient person. In fact he remained working part-time while attending the hospital – significantly he was always self-employed.

It is clear from this material that the ability to work had considerable significance for Ben. When faced with the community working successfully, he felt in some way provoked. An internal object-relation became externalized for him in such a way that he had to establish an image of a community that was not successful and that required criticism from the vantage point of his own wisdom. He was able to externalize his internal relationship with a destroyed object, and to show the reason for his dour life-long work of reparation. He achieved this by making his projection of inexperience (impotence) into the community sufficiently effective to actually bring the community to a halt in its work. He had then externalized his own internal relationship into the actual organization of the community.

E 15.2 **The emotional intruder**

Brenda was a creative young woman (an art student) who suffered from bouts of depression. Shortly after admission to the community she made various forlorn demands – to have individual sessions instead of just small groups, to be admitted to the in-patient unit instead of just attending during the day. It was clear that one of the roots of her demands was a marked susceptibility to feeling excluded. She soon tackled the problem of becoming part of the community meetings – and she did it in her own characteristic way. She put her head in her hands and began crying, sobbing in a heart-rending manner. It was a dramatic gesture which riveted everyone's attention on her. Unlike Ben's interventions in the previous example, which provoked retaliation, Brenda provoked guilty concern. Having gained this rapt attention and a number of paper handerchiefs, she would set off on a woeful account of her failures. When others put in comments, interpretations, or confrontations, she accepted them willingly to add conviction to the general message – 'look how neurotic I am'. In this way she deprived all other comments of any helpful significance. Community meetings would grind to a halt in a state of helpless, frustrated concern and guilt which could not leave the sufferer alone, but could not offer relief.

Later, when her depression had begun to lift she was able, when so moved, to disrupt meetings with the same effectiveness. This time with giggling and laughter. The merriment had an infectious quality which spread to other people so that serious efforts could not easily be returned to. 'What's wrong with a little innocent laughter?' she would ask, thereby only increasing the force of the frustration she was projecting.

Brenda interfered with the community's concern and care for its members. For Brenda, it was related to her identification with her mother who had actually been a refugee (excluded). Yet it also arose from her own experience of exclusion and loss in childhood when mother died after a long illness. In effect Brenda had taken second place to mother's illness.

There was thus an externalization of the internal relations with a dead or dying mother who was too much in need of care herself to be able to care for her daughter. The externalization, however, also expressed the mischievous effort to destroy the caring object, the community (which internally was her destroyed mother).

Brenda, like Ben, clearly dramatized her wish to spoil the thing she wished to be included in. Both dramatized an internal relationship with a damaged, dead or destroyed object – typical of many of the severe character disorders in need of full-time treatment. Both also used their own characteristic technique in this destructive process. Once the intolerable feeling itself – impotence in Ben's case, helpless frustration in Brenda's – was projected it brought the community to a halt with the overwhelming experience of that particular feeling.

Interference by events

Another form of interference is when some event affects the community collectively, so that the shared experience provokes a disruptive reaction.

E 15.3 The Easter disruption

The community meeting on a Friday was normally devoted to discussing members of the community who were noted by the committee for being poor attenders in the current week, or who warranted special concern for some other reason. The committee drew up a 'concern list' each week for this purpose. On this particular occasion, the Friday was in a week following Easter when the hospital had been closed the previous Friday and Monday. The meeting opened with a demand by Beryl that, as the week was short, the concern list should be waived. This Friday she wanted an ordinary meeting – i.e. a free-floating discussion of the sort which happens on each of the other days of the week. This week, then, the concern list seemed to be experienced as preventing attention to important problems which might come up in the ordinary way. Other patients backed the demand. On discussing this a little further, it emerged that there was anxiety about the coming weekend – and a reawakening of feelings about the previous long weekend over Easter.

The sequence had become clear. The disruption of the routine of the community the weekend before was recalled this Friday, and the response was to dramatize a disruption of the routine. It was as if some community authority was being dealt with on the principle 'you disrupted our routine last weekend, we'll disrupt yours this time'. Of course this challenge to a community authority could be self-defeating, leading to insecurity and a spiralling disruption and distress. Symbolically, the dramatization was about the anxiety that 'concern' can so easily be cancelled.

In fact in this instance, the issues involved quickly became clear, the reasons were understood and the meeting could then go back to its Friday routine.

Disruption as team work

Sometimes disruption is orchestrated by the provoking of disruptive people.

E 15.4 Disrupting teamwork

Bess, who was in a hypomanic state, repeatedly occupied the meeting, taking attention away from all other people and topics. She attracted comment and yet made no use of anyone's contributions. The meeting faced the typical dilemma posed by a manic patient. Admiration and a totally committed devotion was demanded to the extent of rendering useless the whole of the time of the meeting. The only alternative seemed to be to turn away and make deliberate attempts to exclude her by attending to something else. However, an uneasy feeling of responsibility and guilt usually prevented this. Any constructive outcome of the meetings was jeopardized by Bess's dominating behaviour. Yet the disruptive forces in the group did not just reside in this one patient. It might be more accurate to regard Bess as an instrument of disruption – one of the resources of the group as a whole. At first sight this patient established a single-handed tyranny, but on closer inspection it became clear that she was not successful unless others in the meeting subtly promoted her hegemony. From time to time they would use this instrument. If she fell asleep, she was prompted with vague questions, or addressed directly, or referred to in some other conversation. her talk would be encouraged with sniggers or laughter, or frankly admired as a necessary gaiety. Even when she was not present she would be mentioned and brought into the conversation – often the memory of her was enough to set up frivolity and disruption.

Bess could be relied on to come to the fore when needed. The encouragement of her by other people was a team effort in disruptiveness. It is a method with an obvious attraction, because it is indirect and is suitable for patients (and staff too) who want to hide their own disruptiveness.

When there is some tension in the community about madness or about going to pieces, this form of teamwork may be prevalent. It implies an agreement that it is one individual who is to be held responsible for the disorder. Who better than a rather manic patient to be responsible for the whole world of the community!

Fragility and fragmentation

In the community of people with recent experience of breaking down and going to pieces themselves, there may be quite determined efforts to externalize relationships of this kind. In E 14.7 in the last chapter ('The special group of students'), a small group was in a fragile state and actually went partially to pieces. Anxiety about fragmentation of the group preceded this. By introjection, the state of the group aroused internal anxieties for the individual about himself.

Fears about the fragmentation of one's own self lie deeply ingrained in the personalities of many disturbed patients. The word 'schizophrenia' literally means a mind in many fragments. Schizoid individuals, particularly, live in an internal world dominated by splintering attacks on the self when intolerable experiences are encountered. The process is akin to splitting. It is a splitting of a multiple kind, leading to a chaotic sense of identity and self, and a destruction of the ability to experience anything very much (see Klein, 1946; and see above, chapter 4).

Community disruptions, through introjection, touch on these frantic internal states and create considerable further anxiety. Seeking then to externalize it again, increasing numbers of anxious individuals project the fragmentation back into the community. The disruption snowballs as more and more people are recruited. Rising frustration and insecurity (internal and external) reach a maddening intensity and are further fed by the fear of madness. An end-stage is reached in group uproar.

When there is a high level of anxiety in the community – and especially if it goes unexpressed – any initial disruption increases tension and a sense of frustration with the organization. Those individuals who find the tension hard to bear become provocative of further tension with overt or subtler forms of disruption. And if acting out through non-attendance is not resorted to, then organized activity is progressively broken up. Decision-making declines until it becomes non-existent, or else arbitrary, impulsive, idiosyncratic and only erratically implemented.

The community as a working concern is dismantled. The end result is fragmentation into a chaotic, anarchic state, an aggregate of fearful individuals who are barely differentiated except through spontaneous idiosyncratic actions or utterances. They remain together through a common identification based on continual projections of a fear of their own fragmentation into the external community.

E 15.5 Ruling fragmentation

Unlike Bess in the last example, Bridget was not an instrument of disruption. She was herself the conductor of the teamwork (a role previously described in E 7.1, 'The schizoid ruler'). In this sense she led the fragmented regime of the community, conducting the instruments among whom, Bess might be one.

Bridget was a young, single woman, exceedingly anxious and with no secure place or identity. She was particularly prominent in the community at a time when it was trying to establish itself anew as a therapeutic community. This was a time of considerable dissension at all levels in the community, and staff were much preoccupied in testing out the nature of the new ideas, what authority and leadership were entailed, and what limits could be applied and experimented with. It was a time of enthusiasm, frustration, contradiction and rivalry. The organization of the community was in the melting pot. It was no coincidence that a personality of Bridget's type should come to the fore. Through the medium of her personality she presented the insecurity, instability, confusion of purposes, and the general feeling of limitlessness. Perhaps above all, with her attitude of relentlessness destruction, she was enabling a dramatization of dismantling the 'internal community'. It is possible that during this phase of renewal there was considerable staff guilt about the dismantling of the previous order in the hospital which had led to this persecuting flood of fragmentation – a kind of sorcerer's apprentice punishment.

Bridget's intense feelings always aroused deep concern in the community and carried with them the anxiety that there was no-one around to help her tolerate them or abate their intensity. She gave the impression of living in a desolate or ruined place, and she seemed to experience the fear that she had already overwhelmed the rescuers she depended on. Her only defence seemed to be withering contempt for the community and its organization and for anyone she might need to turn to. This contempt did indeed seem to emphasise the overwhelming quality of her character. And she would eventually lapse from contempt into an exhausted, empty futility.

In the context of the community at this time she was highly influential, dominating it with the quality of her anxieties and then with her contempt. She advocated an extreme permissiveness and at the same time (or in rapid alternation) she experienced an intense languid despair at the feeble achievements of her permissive regime.

Any aspects of organization which put constraints on individuals were strenuously opposed. The efforts of the committee to organize simple systems for getting the washing up done, for example, were denigrated and over a period of time became half-hearted and ineffective. In particular, any efforts by the staff to defend the timetable and keep the programme in order were derided, and the derision was only interrupted by complaints about boredom and the lack of organized facilities.

The hindrance to anything emerging from the melting pot came from panic at the uncertainty that changes, rival ideas and experimentation promise. Bridget's personality aptly represented these anxieties and at the same time allowed her to create a community in her own image. Her despair at handling her own internal state could be expressed through the medium of despair at the community's fragmentation.

The illustrations in this chapter describe the fragile community. At times the organization is especially vulnerable to disruptive influences. The community organization is then threatened by, and in some circumstances succumbs to, fragmentation. Even the threat of it, in a community of anxious people, raises the anxiety sky-high. By even faltering, the community can trigger off in many members their own nightmares of fragmentation. It is of utmost importance that, in the state occurring in the last example, individuals can use the community as a pool for projecting into. Their worst fears come true are yet not quite the worst if everyone is in the same boat together.

Escape from fragmentation

Considerable effort and ingenuity may be displayed in fending off the threat of this occurrence. In example E 14.7 the student group, when it hit its crisis point, attempted to evade the experience of fragmenting. Before the actual flight of members from the group, there was a brief moment when the group stuck together in a sudden pseudo-unity, a clinging together in order not to rock the boat.

Cohesion in a group is important for two general reasons: One is the group's rational pursuit of its task; the other is a defensive need – because fragmentation, or the threat of it, plays so intrusively upon the internal worlds of the individuals. The defensiveness may be a simple clinging, as mentioned above. The welding of the membership into roles in a dramatization is another more complex form of defensive cohesiveness.

The solidarity of a group has therefore to be examined for the degree to which it is defensive. Like the apparently 'good' group, so the apparently cohesive group needs to be checked for what anxieties may be collectively being evaded. A rigid community may be partly protected from fragmentation. However, it also retains a brittleness which can become a palpable threat of fracture when stresses rise sufficiently.

The multiply split community is a kaleidoscope of mutual projection systems. The myriad of barriers in a fragmented community imply projections of all kinds all over the place, the purpose being to dissipate experience so thinly that it can no longer be painful.

Summary

This chapter has given illustrations of the various forms of disruption which can occur in a vulnerable community. They are visible manifestations of the impaired integration that has been demonstrated when the organization contains barriers arising from defensive mutual projection systems. Such manifestations of fragility and incipient fragmentation arouse deep-seated anxieties in the individuals about going to pieces themselves, and their own lack of integration.

16

The faces of rigidity

This chapter will explore rigid strategies for coping with the threat posed by the state of the community. As well as personal evasion – absenteeism, withdrawal, the reappearance of symptoms – there are also community strategies of evasion. Being defensive they have maladaptive and self-defeating consequences. They result in the evasion of reality through rigidity.

Adhesiveness

The momentary sticking together of the student group in example E 14.7 was an emergency action engaged in collectively in a group atmosphere of intense insecurity. The unity and identification of the members were suddenly remarkable – perhaps comparable with the example of collective projection (E 5.3) because the anxiety was collective.

This is a state of adhesion. The membership is constant and attendance regular. Participation has characteristic forms. Either there are almost no contributions, with many anxious silences but considerable eye contact. Or there is bland and repetitive conversation, stereotyped patterns of interchange, or unenlightened reminiscing about the past of the group. The point seems to be to prevent movement or energy. The heaviness and the apparent lack of activity sometimes make the therapist ask of himself – why do these people come with a devotion which seems to be so unrewarded? It is an experience which it pays to reflect upon. It is as if the behaviour of the group members were motivated by the belief that if anything happens, or anything moves, the whole house of cards will fall down. This dramatization of constancy and inactivity is the collective expression by the group members of their despairing fear of their group fragmenting, and then (by introjection) of their own fragmentation.

Any activity on the part of the therapist, or any attempt to stimulate life, are resisted and neutralized because they threaten what feels to the group like an extremely fragile stability. The emergence of tension in the group may produce strident protests. Movement, life and tension may rock the boat and capsize it. The group members are all in the collective state clinging rigidly as one – rigid with fear one might say.

Bureaucratic rigidity

More differentiated states of rigidity are typical of multi-group systems. The natural divisions stimulate phantasies of possible fragmentation into separate bits. The following is a typical example.

E 16.1 The bureaucratic constitution

At a time when a number of people were leaving the community, including some dominant individuals who were a main support to the organization, a fairly prolonged apathy settled in. Decision-making was laborious and difficult. The community was in need of leaders amongst the patients around whom responsible organization could re-form. Here was a basis for a political life of the community, for discussion, activity and confrontation. However, it wasn't quite like that. Community meetings declined into lengthy silences with staff members trying to provoke discussion. Other groups within the programme were poorly supported. There was an attempt to improve the organization by means of a constitution, but sanctions for non-conformist behaviour caught up in their net an unacceptable number of candidates for summary discharge. It was canvassed particularly by some of the outgoing leaders who wished to leave behind a permanent record of their impact on and contribution to the community.

However, on the community level, this bureaucratic or legalistic rigidity reduced the tension and frustration of personal responsibility for the tasks of the community. It is reminiscent of the solution found by the nurses in the Menzies case study described in chapter 13. One feature was the attempt to deal with some of the members who were not attending regularly. They came to be described by a slogan: 'not using the hospital properly'. This was a phrase which might have had significance if the proper use of the hospital had been defined. However, the point is that this was a moment when there was no clarifying discussion of that kind. The phrase therefore rapidly acquired a hollow ring. It came to indicate that immediate action was prescribed (discharge) rather than an attempt to understand the failure and the context of the community relations at this moment. In fact it led to many discharges of poor attenders who were felt to pose too big a therapeutic problem (compare E 10.1, 'The reign of terror').

At the emotional level, discharging these scapegoats was intended to provide relief – relief from having to face difficulties at a time when the community felt fragile and ineffective because the needed leaders were leaving. It was as if they took the effectiveness of the whole organization with them. However, the relief was transient since in the end failure had to be admitted. It intensified the lost potency of the community. The transient relief which came from ordering the discharges did not long cope with the sense of therapeutic impotence. The dilemma became increasingly acute as they continued. In an effort to halt these discharges from a now dwindling community, a contract was designed which would provide a mechanism for automatic suspension, rather than discharge. In order to cover the difficult situation, it included a complex series of clauses about personal attendance rates.

This pursued the bureaucratic, legal solution. The immediate outcome was that on the first occasion that a member was suspended for infringing all of the clauses, there ensued a bitter debate about the actual nature of the clauses. Eventually, to add insult to injury, it was realized that the contract, although written down, had been lost. This debate occupied a great deal of time. It led to disputatious quarrelling and reached no decision.

Designing a rigid bureaucratic procedure which avoids human error, confrontation and discussion, creates more problems than it solves, uses up more time than it saves, and results in more muddled decision making than might otherwise be the case. It serves as a useful lesson in the problems of the life of the community. Clearly, automatic procedures are very difficult to design. The best that could be hoped for, would be good interpretation of the contract; and that points to the need for a 'legal profession' as an organ of the community, overseeing legal procedures.

The reasons for this bureaucratic impetus came from the anxieties that the community organization might not survive the loss of its leadership. The loss of this cohesive force provoked guilt in those who were leaving and insecurity in those staying. These feelings were evaded by a move to enshrine the past leadership on paper in order to ensure continuity. The second stage of the illustration describes a process in which the community actually did seem to be falling apart, with discharges like bits breaking off in all directions. Once again resort was made to a piece of paper on which could be written an authority that nobody felt able to take on themselves. The dwindling community played further on the members anxieties – provoking guilt about sending some away, anxiety through identifying with those discharged, and insecurity because of the rising spectre of a fragmenting community. The contract was an attempt to deal with all that – by stopping the automatic discharge and removing the guilt from any particular person. In attempting to depersonalize the community and its procedures, it is as if members were able to say, 'don't blame us; they're the rules here'. But in addition, 'we have rules here; don't think that we're sloppy or going to pieces'. The latter sentiment, particularly, is the hallmark of the bureaucratic regime. Painful feelings are evaded by denigrating them and calling them sloppy; and also involved is the denial of the anxiety of fragmenting.

The hallmark of the rigid community is the attempt to develop organization for the sake of it. The reasons for its are firstly to counteract anxiety about the structure dissolving and fragmenting, and the insecurity, guilt and sense of responsibility which goes with the fragmentation. Secondly, it copes with the sense of impotence which arises when faced with the designated task – especially such a difficult one as dealing with human suffering and mental disorder. Rigidity in this aspect embodies a task drift.

Ossification

A related form of rigidity is ossification. The term has been used in a looser way by Roberts (1980) to refer to rigid organizations as a whole. In this account it is taken to refer to a carrying on of old organization when it has no more use. The lack of adaptability to a new situation distinguishes it from bureaucratic forms, which do adapt, if in legalistic ways. Where they are similar is in squeezing out the importance of experience and feeling, especially the fear of going to pieces.

E 16.2 The ossified meeting

A weekly staff meeting known as the admission meeting had been in existence for a number of years and had a specific function to assess new referrals to the day community. On this occasion the meeting took place as usual, people gathered slowly, and it was announced by the member who kept the agenda that there were no items on it this week. Undeterred by this, the meeting did not adjourn. On the contrary it found something to discuss – a young chronic schizophrenic. He attended the hospital irregularly and had been doing so for as long as six years. He was extremely disabled and in the past the hospital had shared the responsibility for managing his life with his mother and friends. A proposal was put forward at the meeting that the hospital should relinquish its share of the responsibility. It was actually put in different terms – that the community should stop colluding with his mother to deny the patient responsibility for himself. The counter-argument was that, whatever had been done in the past, he now needed someone to take responsibility for him.

After about twenty minutes the discussion died down. Another member had arrived late and did have a new referral to be discussed. By now, however, another person had recalled that she had something that she wanted discussed quickly, and she was given the floor. It turned out to be far from quick. One of the women patients had a three and a half year old child whom she had presented to the nursing sister for help to remove the child's contact lens (this example has been described from another angle in E 4.1, 'Splitting off a role'). It had been a prolonged and difficult task, with the child screaming for half an hour and the anxiety of the patient and the nurse rising steadily. There was a long and emotive discussion, the upshot of which was that the child should not have to suffer this kind of trauma, and it was proposed that the prescribing ophthalmologist should be contacted and told of the difficulties. It was agreed that the mother (an intelligent but immature woman) should not pass the burden of this responsibility to the nurses. By the time this was resolved the meeting had only five minutes left to consider the new referral.

Curiously, this meeting took place as usual without an agenda, just because it was meeting. A sense of purpose was so distant that when a new referral eventually was brought forward it could not find a place! Over time, the purpose seemed to have become the task of preserving the meeting. The content of the discussion is interesting. It reflected the staff preoccupations at this time. Both of the absorbing discussions involved 'taking responsibility', or rather passing it away from the community. The first discussion concerned keeping up a hopeless situation which had hung over from the past. No-one, it seemed, was willing to take responsibility for cancelling this formal meeting. The anxiety about holding things together (aggravated by the apparent lack of referrals perhaps) seemed evident. The meeting's way of dealing with this was to avoid the painful and distressing 'contact' reported by the nurse and stick to routine for its own sake. This is the rigid solution, to kill experience and leave the sense of responsibility to pass elsewhere.

Ossification is similar to the clinging described in the first section of this chapter. It is an adhesion to the organization – the structure of the timetable.

The iron fist

Earlier (see Chapter 7 on the regime and the individual), another rigid form of the community was described. The psychopathic leader, of the kind described there, provokes the community which protects itself against the simple enactment of the leader's characteristic object-relations. Instead the community rises to the challenge and dramatizes a protection against it. The iron fist of the community can come down on these personality types and control their excesses. It does so in characteristic ways. Like the bureacratic regime and ossification it is designed to protect against fragmentation. The rigidity of the community regime constructed in response to this kind of personality can be seen when they are concentrated in a therapeutic community.

Highly manipulative, impulse-driven psychopathic personalities come quickly to light in a therapeutic community. And the therapeutic community has, to some extent, created its reputation with psychopaths. Referring to the treatment of prison inmates at Grendon Underwood, Gunn *et al.*, (1978) admiringly say: 'Overall the results tend to emphasise the special benefits of group treatment, especially treatment carried out in a therapeutic community'.

The impact of the psychopath on a community can be very great. A relationship comes to be established between the psychopath and his community in which his manipulations and impulses give rise to increasing aggravation, with an increasingly punitive response. The psychopath exists in relation to an external punitive agent and he establishes this wherever he can. For instance, the rigorous rule-bound toughness and punishment of the normal prison regime is typical of the kind provoked by psychopaths wherever they are. This is the characteristic object-relation of this kind of psychopath; it is a feature of his make-up and the only variant is when at times he can play the part of the bullying punitive agent himself (the gang-leader in prison; or example E 20.1). The psychopath is engaged in a highly defensive operation when he influences the community in his direction. The defensive gain is that, although the external agent comes to exist really for him and he may be really punished, he can take comfort in a private satisfaction that it is a discredited agent. The punishment is unjust and he proves it is the punitive agent who is morally degenerate.

The community at the Henderson Hospital, 'is a very specific model which many have criticised as being too rigid. But in attempting to meet the needs of this particular type of individual for which it has developed its structure the latter has some important purposes and meanings' (Whiteley *et al.*, 1972, p. 40). The particular meaning referred to is that the group has come to dramatize a punitive internal relationship (just as in prison). Because it provides a collective gain (discrediting authority) it can be passed on from one generation of patients to the next. In the course of manipulating his way through this kind of therapeutic community, the individual finds himself elected to official positions within the community. He in his turn becomes a defender of the rigid system and an active controlling agent. Every month new elections take place. There are enough posts for nearly everyone, some of which have great responsibility, and there is a good deal of heirarchical ranking of them. However, the individuals are not simply left to their own devices in this way. The community 'is a continuous, stressful, 24-hour process of self-perception' (Whiteley, 1972). His active object-relationships are presented back to him. What he dramatizes is brought back to him in words. In Whiteley's account, the Henderson Hospital clearly characterizes the relationship between a certain personality type collected together and the rigid community regime. The rigid regime forms out of the most unpromising material – those who might otherwise establish a personal hegemony for their own whims.

Complexity

Both the accretion of bits and pieces of organization and the clinging on to every aspect of the old structure (rigid bureaucracy and ossification respectively) contribute to a phenomenon in which complexity relentlessly increases. This occurs in a community situation when there is too much anxiety for the kind of radical rethinking which is necessary to keep the community adapted to its current tasks. It is therefore not simply a feature of large and complicated organizations alone. Complexity evolves in small communities under the pressure of anxiety about the organization itself. There is too much doubt to allow questioning and adaptation to develop. One feature of this organizational dinosaur is that the proliferating parts fail to hold together in the absence of good communication. Barriers exist in all directions.

E 16.3 Complexity

Roughly three and a half to four years after the attempt to institute rigorous therapeutic community principles, the community began to develop quite fast. New ideas for specific therapeutic foci within the community were being put forward. New groups and structures were evolving; a dream group, a representative group for meeting 'suspended' patients, a leavers' group, the admission of patient representatives to staff meetings. The rapidity of development was exhilarating, and seemed to indicate a gathering liveliness in the community. However, there were some untoward developments at the same time. A period of delinquent behaviour set in on an unprecedented scale. There were thefts, a pregnant member of staff was physically assaulted and an unknown member of the community began fire-setting. Complaints were voiced directly that not enough attention was being paid to the community as a whole, that there were too many separate, disparate groups.

Above all, the community meetings became progressively unforthcoming, sullen and oppressive. If the community was actually livelier, it wasn't apparent from the community meetings. They were especially characterized by a listless apathy which we christened 'the large group syndrome' (Hinshelwood and Grunberg, 1975). During this time, the staff group itself contained the individual enthusiasms that the separate members were engaged in when they ran their groups and events in their programme. However, there was a lack of support for each others' projects, an impatience about listening to others' work, and the general absence of a cohesive team.

At one point a member of staff made a complaint about having a special dream group. It detracted from other groups if dreams were saved for working at in an exclusive dream group. Sides were taken. Discussion broadened within the staff group. It came to be recognized that there was difficulty in passing information from the members of one activity in the programme to those in another. Members of staff involved in one group, it was realized, were often not aware of what was happening in other groups and activities. The difficulty in passing on information was partly due to the steady proliferation of new activities. However, this was by no means the whole explanation, for difficulty was actively experienced in managing the daily feedback reports. Exchange was just not taking place. It was possible to talk things over only in sub-groups of staff. Everything had 'sub-grouped', and there were barriers in all directions.

Subsequent to this hesitant realization, signs of more open conflict developed between the different therapeutic approaches – roughly speaking, between the formal, verbal, psychoanalytically-based psychotherapy on the one hand and newer methods such as encounter or bioenergetics on the other.

This example brings together three components: (i) the lively development which may or may not represent a community in good heart; (ii) a behavioural disturbance which suggested strongly that the liveliness was only one side of the story; (iii) a seriously debilitated, fragmented community meeting which seemed to confirm that the state of the community required urgent attention.

Much of this derived from rivalry between staff (see chapter 8 on staff as the transference object), but much can also be put down to personal doubt. Demoralization and personal doubt were dealt with by each individual becoming sealed in his own personal support system, protected from knowing about others' good efforts. The increasing diversification of treatment groups arose partly for reasons of personal protection, and the sub-group of staff became a support system against the fear that someone else would show you up in your own efforts. This had occurred without design, and without being recognized until it was upon us. Open conflict and rivalry had been averted – but at a price. The price was the projection of personal doubt and ineffectiveness into someone else's part of the system, into someone else's work. These mutual projections then became multiple barriers to the exchange of information and the result was the distorted importance given to the separate parts of the system. One could say the part was more than the whole – this is the hallmark of complexity, and may be observed, for example, in the account of the large mental hospital as a demoralized organization given in chapter 11 above.

The broken community

The most characteristic feature of the rigid organization is its attitude to change. The individuals sense that they are caught in an immovable system which feels quite unresponsive – faceless. The roles and even the opinions required of them seem unyielding to the person's individuality.

Perhaps it is a familiar experience to leave a group, feeling fully involved and in agreement with what had been decided on or arranged, only to find that in another context the decisions and arrangements appear short-sighted, ill thought-out, ill-informed or even downright wrong. This experience of the loss of one's own judgement and integrity is very painful. To invest oneself in something which turns out to be unreliable results in personal doubt and confusion. Such is the power of a group over its members' ability to think and judge. It is a very great hardship to be caught up in these group processes, yet it is even more unpleasant to stand out against them. Groups act and behave with an almost delusional certainty.

The rigid organization is in fact brittle, as in the last example on complexity. It is not immune from fracture. In contrast to the experience of the individual in a fragile organization, the individual in the rigid one is held secure within his own fragment. Yet he is faced with a multi-group system in which his involvement in the groups results in his unwittingly losing perspective and failing in judgement, especially about the effectiveness of 'his own group' compared with that of others. He is equally unwitting in his acceptance of grossly distorted evaluations of his personal contribution and that of others. In return, he gains some relief from his fear of a sinking ship, and can fancy his own triumphal survival from the general flood of madness and collapsing order. This is comparable to the myth of the community as paradise, where the community is a haven of perfection and peace in the surrounding gloom and hostility. In this case it is the smaller island, the sub-group, which resscues him from the surrounding broken community.

When the broken community comes together again in the community meeting, it is clearly heading for trouble. The individuals, shorn up in their own self-supporting groups, face a breakdown of that system. The individuals are threatened with the loss of their sense of relief and risk coming to doubt their own judgement. In these conditions the community meeting suffers. Open communication fades away very rapidly. In effect the process dramatizes the lack of communication through the silence, listlessness, and evident disengagement. The immediate impression, however, for the individuals in these meetings is once again one of a community which is failing, and this drives further the personal need for support. We are back with a community trapped in a cycle of demoralization. (For a more extensive example of an institution subject to this fate, see the report on the demoralization of a traditional mental hospital in Hinshelwood, 1979.)

Summary

Owing to the deep-seated nature of the anxiety about fragmenting, intense efforts are made to establish protective measures against the disorganization of the community. These rigid defences on a collective scale are various and ingenious. They are not, however, immune from breaking apart down the fracture lines of the structure, which become similar barriers to communication and associated projection systems, resulting in a peculiar bewilderment for the individual members.

17

Dimensions of the community personality

In his famous paper on oscillations in therapeutic communities (1956), Rapoport described a sinusoidal curve like that shown in Figure 17.1. It represents a rise and fall in the cohesiveness of the organization. The resilience of the community copes with intermittent disruptions of various kinds.

Manning (1980) discussed the interacting internal and external factors involved in the intermittent collective disturbances in institutions. In writing about the eventual demise of this community, I stressed the malignancy of unresolved leadership problems (1980). Van Kalsbeck (1980) discussed a similar malignant leadership problem in terms of the conflicting ideology of a new leader with his remaining staff. Kernberg reflected on the personality aspects of the leader:

> *The more severe the leader's personality pathology and the tighter the organisational structure, the greater are the destructive effects of the leader on the organisation. It might be that, under extreme circumstances, the paranoid regression of an entire society maintains the sanity of the tyrant, and, when his control over that society breaks down he becomes psychotic: the final months of Hitler point to this possibility.*   (1984, p.13)

Baron's study (1984) may also point to this.

It is possible to overstress the effects of staff pathology, and of the leader's in particular. Rapoport identified, particularly, the regular occurrence of leading personalities (patients as well as staff – the culture carriers) leaving the community. And Mendizabal (1985) discussed the problems absorbed into a community from a national economic crisis.

Whatever the precursors and causes of a crisis in the group or community, from within or from without, there seem to be two possible responses. The notion of oscillation suggests a certain amount of resilience, or bounce, in the community which has resources for recovery.

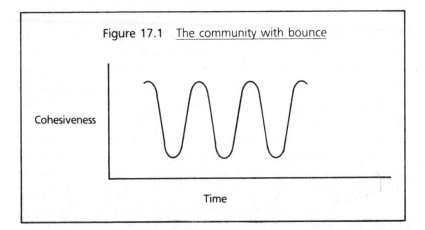

Figure 17.1   The community with bounce

In the preceding chapters we have been concerned with a different kind of community response. When morale is low there is not the same bounce as that detected by Rapoport. Like a ball with a puncture, some communities may fall flat, and stay there (see Figure 17.2).

The demoralization trap

The cylical processes involved in keeping the flat community flat, were formalized above (see chapter 11 on morale and demoralization). They operate to keep the community at a low ebb. Personal and community factors feed into each other and create a persistent atmosphere of low personal confidence and self-esteem, low belief in the effectiveness of

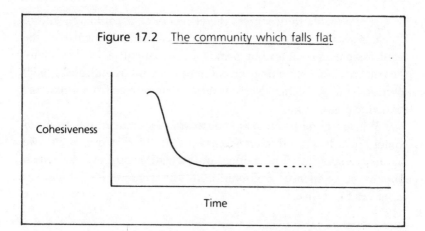

Figure 17.2   The community which falls flat

Cohesiveness

Time

the community, and wild off-target attempts to achieve some aim effectively – which inevitably fail. The community becomes stuck in a demoralization trap. At this point the usual indicators of demoralization appear – absenteeism, high sickness rates, leaving, increased friction. The really telling development, however, is the change in the attitudes of the individuals – typically a dry and humorous lack of respect for the institution emerges. The latter's failings become a major topic and a source of funny stories. There is a frank disbelief and cynicism about anything which goes right; and eventually a growing bitterness about the general frustrations and the individual's helplessness. It becomes increasingly difficult to hold an attitude of respect towards the institution, and the individual who tries to be respectful finds himself the butt of his colleagues' humour. Eventually a competitive trade in defamatory stories about the institution grows up (see Hinshelwood, 1979). Details of these attitudes of the demoralization trap are described extensively in chapter 11, and also in the illustrations of the more extreme states of demoralization, E 7.1, 'The schizoid ruler', and E 15.5, 'Ruling fragmentation' (see also the description of the demoralized organization in chapter 11).

The development of cynicism and scepticism makes this process extremely difficult to reverse. The organization remains floundering with morale at rock bottom. Mutual support of a personal nature between close colleagues often runs high in the face of this adversity. Yet, although the institution may be regarded as a friendly place, this depends on the shared humour and shared bitterness at the organization's expense, and at the expense of its reputation with its members.

The demoralization trap is a self-perpetuating cycle (a positive feedback system) characteristic of this kind of flat community. The end result is not necessarily complete dissolution. Manning (1980), for instance, suggests an analogy with the human organism in which there is a stage of functional or social death before the biological death. The community may die functionally without being dissolved physically. We have witnessed this functional death in the many vicious circles described in chapters 11 and 12. It provokes many efforts collectively to avoid awareness of it. Thus chronic states of fragmentation and demoralization can exist indefinitely – for example when there is no alternative institution to take over the task of the one which is failing. The traditional mental hospital exists in a permanent state of functional death (Hinshelwood, 1979) and yet it remains needed because of its complicated function within society at large (Bott, 1976). The organization develops its own rigid defensiveness. Goffman (1961) gave the classical account of this awful culture. Others (for instance, Stanton and Schwartz, 1954, or Rosenberg, 1970) are less one-sided in their analysis of the defensive systems of inmates and staff.

The fragile community

Therapeutic communities, too, can go seriously wrong. Baron's study of a community fragmenting and undertaking frail efforts to bring the situation under control, describes the details of this process (1984; 1987). Anzieu (1984) in studying groups from a psychoanalytic point of view, regards the phantasy of the group falling apart as one of the key elements in group life. Springman (1976) described the fragmentation of the large group as a defensive manifestation against the anxiety of the largeness of the large group. The anxiety about fragmentation and the possible defensive manoeuvres to which it might be put, come out in the arena of the community as actual processes in which the community does begin to go to pieces, and sets up a tension between centripetal and centrifugal forces. The threat of the fragile community to shatter into fragments, and the rigid community struggling against fragmentation, are dimensions that could be used for systematic descriptions of communities and groups. They give rise to basic types of community arising out of the present observations.

A typology of communities

Some of the factors can be represented in graph form. Figure 17.3 shows how the community with bounce varies along two dimensions. At times when something disturbs the community organization (along the horizontal axis in Figure 17.3) the cohesiveness falls steadily down the slope of the line. If the disturbance reduces (to the left on dimension D) the community regains cohesiveness (up on dimension C), and the pattern would revert to that shown in Figure 17.1. For instance, in Rapoport's example the community was disturbed particularly by the departure of staff or patients – and presumably also by the admission of new patients (more disturbance). As the disturbance increased the community would slide down the curve. But it was a resilient community that could slide back up again as the disturbance became contained.

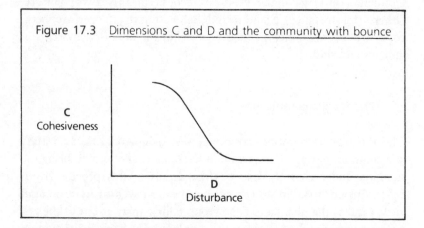

Figure 17.3   Dimensions C and D and the community with bounce

C
Cohesiveness

D
Disturbance

However, there is a different state of affairs with the community which falls flat (see Fig. 17.4).

The dimensions are the same as in the previous figure, but the curve is different. As the disturbance increases along dimension D – say from position b to position a – there is a precipitous drop on to the lower arm of the curve. This lower arm represents the lost cohesiveness and therefore means fragmentation. The important thing is that the community cannot simply reverse this. If disturbance diminishes, the community remains trapped on the lower arm. It is only when it gets a long way back that it could then 'fall' upwards to

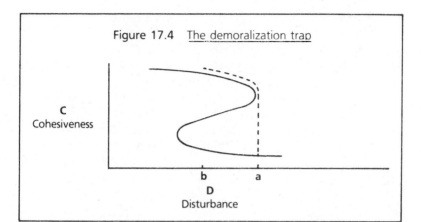

Figure 17.4   The demoralization trap

C
Cohesiveness

b   a
D
Disturbance

the upper arm again and regain its integrity. As we have seen, especially in chapter 11, the fall from grace itself increases fears and therefore the amount of disturbance. So the fall itself makes it even more improbable that the community could get far enough back along dimension D to become reintegrated.

The properties of the two different kinds of community are expressed in these two graphs. From the point of view of managing the community, if it is in a fragile condition or framented, the important question is how to move towards the community with bounce. If we link the two curves from Figures 17.3 and 17.4 by adding another dimension we have a curve in three dimensions. It is a folded sheet drawn using perspective (Fig. 17.5). The third dimension is labelled simply 'F' for the moment.* The nearest edge of the sheet follows the curve of Figure 17.4 which depicts the behaviour of the flat community. A similar precipitous fall happens from the upper leaf, X, at the point where the sheet folds under and the community ends up in a similar demoralization trap between Y and Z.

Now that we have introduced a third dimension, it would be theoretically possible for the community to find another way out of the trap at Z. If it could move backwards along dimension F towards position W at the back of the figure, the demoralization trap fades out. The community would then have achieved a more resilient form which does not get trapped in the demoralization spirals. This theoretical possibility is examined in the next chapter.

*The graphs in this section (Figures 17.3 to 17.5) are adapted from Postle (1980), while Figure 17.6 in the following section is taken directly from Postle.

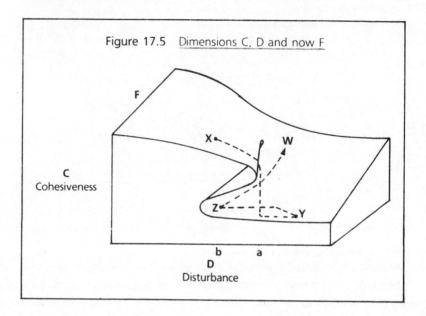

Figure 17.5 Dimensions C, D and now F

Rigidity

We know that rigid forms of community integrity are another means by which the fragmented state can be avoided. We can create a further dimension for this – dimension R. To represent this fourth dimension it is necessary to draw a series of three dimensional figures across the page like a film strip (see Fig. 17.6, p. 213) As the figure progresses across the page the fold in the sheet progresses too. It moves along dimension D as the figure moves along dimension R. The position of the fold can be emphasized for clarity by drawing its 'shadow' on to the base of the solid figure. The triangular 'shadow' is called the cusp. On the left of Figure 17.6, the fold is shown at a very low disturbance mark. This represents the community as particularly fragile since it crashes down on to the lower leaf at very low levels of disturbance. The right-hand side of Figure 17.6 indicates high rigidity, and we see that it takes very high levels of disturbance before the community falls on to the bottom leaf. However, nowhere on dimension R does the front edge lose its fold, and at high levels of R the fragile community only turns into a brittle one. We can also note that the alternative route backwards along dimension F remains open at all levels of R.

Rigidity offers itself, as we have seen in the examples of the last chapter, as the protection against the threat of fragmentation. However, it is only a relative protection and it carries with it the pernicious disadvantages of the depersonalization and institutionalization

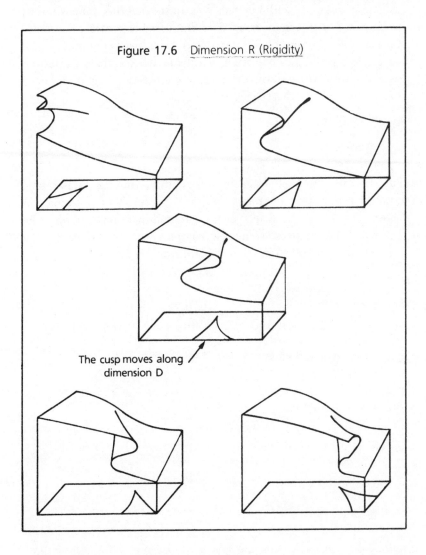

Figure 17.6   Dimension R (Rigidity)

The cusp moves along dimension D

of the members; a diminished capacity to judge reality; and the distortion of the community task towards something which appears superficially more attainable.

The flexible community

Movement backwards over the folded sheet remains the most suitable solution to the organizational problems. It is a movement towards a resilient community with bounce. We can see that this dimension (F) is concerned with a movement between a fragile/brittle community and a flexible community. The flexible end signifies a community with low distortion of communication; a realistic belief in the organization (morale); a resilience to disturbance; and a careful adaptation of the community to stick close to its proper task.

Summary

The interplay between fragility and rigidity, and the catastrophic sense of community fragmentation, are the result of a number of factors. These can be displayed as a four-dimensional graph. The features of this graph are somewhat complex since they represent the cyclical events involved in the demoralization trap.

PART V

Therapy in the community

18

The importance of dimension F

We have seen that derivatives of the individual's object-relations merge in unconscious aspects of the interpersonal relations of the community. This interpenetration of the social and the individual is of high theoretical interest, but it is above all therapeutically very important.

It is not a one-way process. Through projection and introjection the internal world colours the community personality; and the community personality modifies the individual's internal world.

In part IV we saw the demoralization trap and the cyclical processes which sustain it. The problem was to find a point of entry into the cycle. Simply making structural changes in the community organization is not enough. This is the strategy of the rigid community (bureaucratic legalism, complexity). We need to understand how to change the human folkways by which the system is worked. It is the whole system of attitudes, dramatizations and their context in the community which needs a strategy.

The key to this change is movement on dimension F (from position Z to position W in Figure 17.5). This move is not related to the amount of disturbance in the community (dimension D), nor is it influenced by rigidity (dimension R). F is a long-term factor, much as a mood is longer-term than an emotion. The degree of flexibility of a particular therapeutic community could be thought of as a coefficient of therapy. The more flexible the community, the better the chance of modifying (through introjection) the individual's internal world in the direction of a more flexible one.

What then is dimension F? And how can a community be influenced to move along it? The clinical features of F can be summarized in terms of: (i) the ability to verbalize rather than dramatise issues; (ii) a sustained and realistic belief in the effectiveness of the organization; (iii) the ability to face the worst and thus to stick to the task without drifting; (iv) a relative freedom from barrier-formation and its characteristic mutual projection system.

In order to describe the clinical features involved in movement along dimension F, I shall use an example in which a fundamental problem of the community's integrity was tackled. The early poor attempts can be compared with the more successful later ones. In the course of this example I shall comment on some major factors:

1   the projective system (handling the sense of responsibility);
2   community issues (and in this case the manner in which the community sets about trying to change the structure which threatens to fragment);
3   the task and the confrontation with the community's effectiveness (suitability for treatment);
4   facing the worst fears ('some of us may not be able to be helped');
5   the place of leadership (verbal/dramatizing);
6   communication around splits (barriers) in the community.

One of the conclusions to be drawn from this example is the importance of the management of responsibility – how, for instance in non-flexible organizations responsibility is misperceived, mishandled and coped with by means of projection. The various forms of guilt, blame and responsibility are felt to be torturing in the manner described in chapter 4, and the experience is disposed of in characteristic manner through projection into someone else who is supposed to end up experiencing it. Such passing the buck is less pernicious in a more flexible organization.

The example starts with just such batting back and forth between patients and staff. This kind of interchange is also illustrated in E14.8 ('The emotional hot potato'). The efforts were eventually successful but entailed a splitting of the patient group, with one side forming an alliance with the staff as a means of deciding on the issue of who is suitable for treatment (see also E12.1, 'Rescuing morale' and E20.1, 'Therapy is a community process').

Movement on dimension F

E 18.1 Tackling the attendance problem

Early in the history of the development of this therapeutic community its culture had to depart from that of the previous run-down regime. There had been a tendency for a significant proportion of patients to attend irregularly and infrequently. They were mainly people who had come to the community a long time ago and were hanging on now for no very clear reason. Attendance, non-attendance, length of stay, leaving, and absence of a sense of purpose, were rarely discussed openly in the community and were difficult to bring to the community's attention. If they were thought to be important by some, these issues could only be attended to briefly and dismissed (this is described in more detail in E 5.4, 'The community as paradise').

The first move in sorting out responsibility for attendance was to keep bringing it into the community discussion. Attendance is an ever-present problem, actual or potential, for a day community. The solidarity, integrity and cohesiveness of the community is very dependent on the members turning up regularly and punctually. Conversely, absence and unpunctuality provide good opportunities for acting-out which have a major impact on the rejected fragmented community.

The staff began with a concerted effort to bring these issues to the attention of the community meetings. They began focussing down on the here and now, on each individual's record of attendance and participation in the meetings themselves. There was, however, a certain air of unreality about a discussion about attendance at a meeting in which there was such a high rate of non-attendance that the main culprits were never present.

The major sequel to this move was a steady decline in the attendance at community meetings. The worsening problem then led to a decision to move the community meeting. Instead of being first thing in the morning it was timed for around lunchtime. It was supposed that more patients would be in for the meal and could therefore be caught for the meetings!

The time of the community meeting was changed for reasons which have a certain logic. It is, however, a misplaced logic which does not link itself to the therapeutic use of the issue. It is a kind of 'surface' logic which slides off causes and does not really get to grips with the problem. Starting with the individuals' problems led to missing the important community factor. Changing the time of the meeting was bowing before a mightier force, but a force which was not defined or understood. These structural changes were themselves based on dramatizations – the weakness and ineffectiveness of the community were being dramatized and the casual attitude to the meeting time dramatized the flimsy and flabby integrity of the organization. In practice, therefore, the decision only played into the dramatization. It was therefore doomed. The staff were partly aware of that as we shall see.

The decision, made by such of the community as bothered to turn up, was not easily accepted by many of the staff who felt it to be a defeat. In addition, those staff who now ran activities first thing in the morning when the meeting used to be, were especially affected and demoralized by the inherited poor attendance. Life in the community meetings at the later time did not improve. A slightly improved attendance was offset by increasing mutism and apparent sullenness.

A good deal of further discussion by the staff took place. After some time, the staff unilaterally reversed the decision and placed the meetings back as the first event each day. This second decision, representing the staff getting tough, fared no better than the first. Attendance in the morning remained abysmally low.

The community was still thrashing about in the demoralization trap. The dramatizations were still not being understood. The staff continued to dramatize the role of weak authorities in charge of an ineffective community. In spite of the move to make them look instantly strong and to improve staff morale, it only put things back at square one. It was still not appreciated that the problem was to engage the responsibility of the patients in a joint exercise. It was not appreciated that the patients were able to avoid their own responsibility in both the first and second decisions. In the first one, those patients actually present could feel a regret that someone else had defeated the community, while they themselves were not responsible. In the second decision, once again the patients could retreat into the view that the poor staff were getting anxious about something, and once again the responsibility for the meeting was taken out of their hands by the staff's unilateral decision.

The staff, however, were able to have another go, this time with more circumspection and greater attention to the dynamics. They were more successful. The staff again took the initiative and, working at first on their own, produced specific proposals which were put forward as suggestions rather than as authorizations. The staff were quite explicit that they had lost faith in the patients being able to help fully in the struggle to sort out the problem from scratch. Therefore the staff took the first steps. Their leadership, however, fell short of complete and unilateral control of the community. The staff's suggestions were haggled over for some time and there were heated discussions (unusual for this period) which led to an eventual vote accepting the staff's proposals.

The staff were now taking a different form of leadership. They did not just interpret to individuals, thus neglecting the community issues and the associated projective systems. Nor did they make virility-enhancing proclamations. Instead something different happened. While acknowledging their own responsibility in getting the community out of the dismal morass, they were also able to put across proposals in such a way as to invite a partnership – initially at least in the form of a vote. Although there was considerable discussion amongst the patients over whether they were being condescended to, or alternatively being rapped over the knuckles (both representations of a passive passing of the responsibility buck), the majority did in fact accept a share in the responsibility. What was happening, then, was the following. In the earlier course of this problem the responsibility for the problem was felt and held entirely by the staff. The patients could project their sense of responsibility away from themselves into the staff group. Such a projection then induced the communication problems and the jaded beliefs in the community effectiveness. However, through sharing, the staff were able to get the patients to take back some of the sense of responsibility. This gentler 're-projection' by the staff, was now matched by a willingness on the part of the majority of patients to introject and begin to dismantle the communication barriers (resulting from projected responsibility and guilt) between staff and patient. The staff had managed to avoid the nasty pitfall of overloading the patients with a sense of responsibility which would feel just too much to shoulder and would then be swiftly dealt with by means of further projection.

The actual proposal presented by the staff was that a community register be kept and examined each week to discuss those members whose attendance stuck out as worst. They were to be discussed in terms of their commitment to this kind of therapeutic regime. And if it was felt that anyone's commitment was in doubt, he could be temporarily suspended from the community and transferred to a twice weekly 'suspension' group (later renamed the 'concern' group). What was here being propounded was (a) that clinical discussions and doubts about suitability for treatment were responsibilities of the whole community working jointly; (b) that non-conformity, at least in attendance, was a clinical problem about motivation and commitment, and that this was also a community responsibility to be investigated and organized for.

A fresh breeze of reality blows through this development. The matter of who is treatable and who is not was being faced; and the previous notion that someone could remain indefinitely and with only minimal commitment was being firmly put into question. It is at some point every patient's fear that he may not be successfully treated. The staff faced this fear with a certain strength, with the result that confidence in the staff and the commnity rose. The staff also faced the equally nasty notion of having to say 'no' to certain people. Regret and guilt might increase but it was only a partial 'no' – a suspension in order to provide an opportunity to face a realistic purpose. Even if the wildest hopes could not be achieved, patients were not alone with their failure and disappointment.

There was, nevertheless, a whole catalogue of responses to the staff's proposals. On the staff side, the suggestions were justified by the following mixed bag of arguments: it would break the patients' bad habit of sleeping late; patients would be pushed into taking responsibility for themselves and for the community; the hospital would become less slack, less of a drop-outs' paradise; hitherto unnoticed problems would come out into the open through examining the acting-out. The patients met this enthusiasm negatively as well as positively. There were accusations that the individual would be lost in the system or the bureaucracy; the 'community' did not exist anyway because it was nothing like a real community; the hospital, or staff, were naturally punitive, if not downright sadists/fascists/gestapo, etc. Equally, there was the wish to go along dependently with the 'all-powerful' staff.

Yet, although the staff and patients put forward arguments laced with residual myths and dramatized roles, there was eventually a sense of responsibility solid enough to form a partnership to make the hospital more effective; to accept a minimal degree of commitment; to be willing to see the overall task as an examination of the relationships which the individuals made with the community.

The split amongst the patients polarized fairly swiftly after that. One side recognized that the community had to start working better, for everbody's sake; and the other side held that in the process some people would suffer. These facts were difficult to keep together. In the course of discussions these views had to be integrated.

Once these splits were out in the open in words, they could be argued through. The heated quality of the discussions was a clear sign of a community in which entrenched positions had been loosened and hitherto dramatized issues were coming to be verbalized. The staff were able to work together over this – both in their prior discussions and in working it through with the whole community. This experience of working together gave them heart. Witnessing the staff working together effectively began to restore a sense of security for the patients. A benign circle began to operate (see Fig. 12.5). The community had become accessible to change and adaptation once again. These later moves were radically different from the earlier defensive decision-making. It is therefore to be regarded as a shift along dimension F, towards the flexible end.

The features of dimension F

In the above example the community did not simply improve its organization – it improved the way it went about improving its organization. At first the community was handicapped in hidden ways. It could not right the faults that were obvious to all. There was then a significant shift in the community personality towards the flexible end of the dimension.

Various features of flexibility come out of this example.

Projection: The initial projection system was fierce and crippling. It allowed no real change, apart from inadequate 'surface' change. Responsibility was massively projected into someone else: sometimes by the patients into the staff, who were cripplingly burdened by it; or into circumstances which seemed to enforce acquiescence (such as changing the meeting time to lunchtime).

That was the fragile end of dimension F. Later on the situation was more flexible. The projections were handled differently. A gentle re-projection of the disowned responsibility was made by the staff back to the majority of the patients. It had then lost its crippling quality and could be owned.

Community issues: The issue was originally seen as the individual's personal problem in getting to the meeting. This simplistic location of the problem lost sight of the community. Group dynamics remained unaltered and were potentially just as crippling. The individual remained locked in his own isolated fragment of 'community'. This was defensive in that it avoided looking at the ragged community organization and the hopes it had shattered. It also emphasized the individuals as being larger than the community, and protected their narcissism.

Later, a more complex understanding developed. The individual was not isolated from the community issue. He may have his problems, but by membership of the community he made them community issues as well, and the community had to shoulder the problem and organize for it. Absenteeism was something to do with the individual but it was equally a community problem; which in turn created a problem for the individual, thus forming a vicious circle. Progress was made only when the genuinely communal nature of the problem was accepted.

The task: The community task had originally got lost under the dust of years of a run-down regime. The idea of therapeutic success has been fudged in practice and there was no consensus at all on how it could be achieved. In the fragmented community the task was unclear, or unrealistic (usually omnipotent), or had been changed out of all recognition. Believing it might be therapeutic simply to change the time of the meeting to lunchtime (or back again) was a complete misjudgement of the task. There may indeed be good therapeutic reasons for such a change. The problem was that it ignored a therapeutic process.

Later, in order to increase flexibility, one essential ingredient was to face the realistic therapeutic task and boil it down to an operational policy – who should leave (be suspended) from the community.

The task initially was conceived in unrealistic terms. There was a persistent blind spot around the detrimental effects of absenteeism on the individual and the community. It was then matched by unrealistic expectations – for instance, the belief that the staff could deal with the problem by means of simple proclamation.

Equally striking were the painful consequences, during the later flexibility, when individuals were confronted with the reality of their failures. The community had to take its courage in its hands and start to face these awful human problems, and its own limitations.

Worst fears: The projection systems of the fragile community are the individual's escape routes from his own worst fears. However, the therapeutic community has no greater purpose than to find less defensive means of coping with these fears. The flexible community is one which in some measure can confront these anxieties even when the individual cannot. In particular by containing these anxieties in verbal discussion in the community the individual could, by means of introjection, begin to develop a more flexible organization of defences within himself.

Leadership: The example nicely demonstrated different styles of leadership. First, the staff led weakly – by offering individual interpretations to people who often were not present, by capitulating to circumstances and by leaving the practical situation to be managed by those with least authority. Reacting against this, the staff then led by means of rigid authoritarian proclamation, with a similar forlorn result. This was an attempt to protect the community by a move on dimension R, and was a diversion from the task of therapeutic investigation.

Later, the leadership could engage the followers as partners, and together mount a more fervent respect for reality and the task. While accepting the existence of a dramatization, the staff did not go along with it. Intuitive leadership often understands this and will be blessed by the community for being able both to embody and to transcend the dramatized roles – a form of leadership that is referred to as charismatic. Therapeutic communities seem to be especially favourable soil for the blooming of charisma (Rose, 1982). But more therapeutic benefit would come from a fully conscious and verbal understanding of the dramatization to be dealt with.

Barriers: Splits within the community become barriers driven by the defensive needs of the individuals. In the early state in the example, the splits endured as blocks and a distortion of communication which threatened to fragment the system.

The flexibility entailed bridging these barriers and allowed a direct and undistorted expression of the mutual suspicion and hostility. The leadership must be able to speak equally to both sides without attacking the dramatization and thus become embroiled in it.

This bridging function is a crucial therapeutic factor since by means of introjection, it may lead to the internal healing of splits (see chapter 20).

The individual's own flexibility

A great deal of emphasis has been put, in all these examples, on the way personal anxieties and their defences flesh out the bones of the organizational skeleton. These are the 'human folkways by which the system is worked' of which Main speaks.

Furthermore the community which can move itself away from fragmentation and rigidity towards flexibility can enable the patient to take into himself the capacity to move himself away from his defensive evasions towards a more flexible attitude to his own experience and anxiety.

Rigid defensiveness and going to pieces are community problems which, through the to-and-fro process of projection and introjection, the individual can feel very personally. The community's struggles come to be his own. He has to struggle inside himself to move from his own fragility towards a flexibility; and a community which can deal openly with communal problems, including the community problem of what to do with him, will strengthen the individual's own efforts. A community which spends its time puzzling over its own splits, and how to bridge them, will strengthen the individual in his efforts to puzzle over his own splits and how to integrate himself.

The individual needs to identify with a therapeutic community rather than a defensive community.

The collective management of responsibility

The relationships between individuals, and between groups, exist as models for internal integration between parts of an individual's personality. In the community the individual will come to talk things over with himself, in a mode that resembles the kinds of communications exemplified in the community.

The example in this chapter has illustrated two different styles of relationships – and the movement from one to the other. The relationships dealt with the placing of responsibility. In the fragile or fragmented style responsibility was projected into anyone and everyone else.

This need to project responsibility is bound up with the way in which it is experienced. Chapter 4 described the nature of this intense and intolerable guilty responsibility. And it has been clear from many examples that responsibility is often felt to be cripplingly burdensome, so much so that instead of leading to realistic activity, it can lead to paralysis interspersed with erratic and extravagant impulses to omnipotence.

The helplessness, the unreality and the wholesale unloading of responsibility are characteristic distortions which are very prevalent in therapeutic (and other) organizations. As models for introjection they are disastrous. The therapeutic potential lies in a sharing of the projection so that the individual is not alone in facing the unfaceable. He can then introject the sense of being strengthened and accompanied through his worst fears. If the person feels that somebody has stood by him in the external community, he can come to a greater confidence inside himself about standing up to his own scorching sense of responsibility.

Summary

The analysis of community processess into four significant factors has emphasized the importance of dimension F for therapeutic purposes. The features of flexibility, illustrated in E. 18.1 comprise: controlled re-projection, communal issues, the realistic task, facing worst fears, the leader in a partnership, and bridging splits. There are important implications here for the management of structural changes in the community, for the style of leadership employed by the staff, and for the realistic distribution of responsibility.

19

The community personality as container

Through the process of externalizing into dramatizations the community comes to 'contain' the individual. It is asked to contain that aspect of his personality that he feels least able to contain in himself.

Where there is a preponderance of one certain kind of individual the community personality will approximate towards some common denominator. That is to say, it will tend towards a pure culture of the dominant internal object-relations expressed as dramatizations in the style of the organizational regime and in the community meetings. For example, the dramatization of personal and – by externalization – social fragmentation is especially familiar in a community of schizoid and borderline personalities.

The patient needs a secure community environment into which he can project his insecurities. Communities can then contain these projections either well or poorly. In the last chapter we discerned the ingredients of a move from doing it poorly to doing it well – a move along the F dimension.

We have dwelt on communities which show 'a pathology of their own'. They also break down. As we have seen, this is complex since the community problems are, in turn, often promoted by the internal fears of the individuals. By means of projection the fears flesh out the structure of the community with their own morose expectations.

Container and contents

This book has been very largely concerned with the transportation of stressful experiences between people. A major concept which helps us to think about this kind of dynamic is that of the 'container'. The concept actually came from observations of the kind which have been described here (for example, E 5.3, 'A collective projection'). Projective identification is the phantasy that an actual part of one's self has been removed to some other person, who now contains it. This deeply unconscious and rather bizarre thought was first described by Klein (1946), but has been elaborated since, particularly by Winnicott (for example, 1960) and Bion (1961, 1970). The model is the baby whose mental state is 'contained' by the mother. Imagine a baby who is hungry. At the age of a few days he is hardly capable of understanding his own needs and bodily sensations. What he does is cry. That impinges on mother and she feels his distress. She herself will identify what he needs and will feed him. If she has understood correctly he will feel satisfied.

In the course of time he will begin to understand for himself that when he gets certain sensations from his tummy they get satisfied by mother feeding him. Something important has happened. As well as taking in food, the baby has also accumulated some understanding inside him. Something of mother's mental ability has been introjected (mentally taken in) by the baby who can then use the understanding for himself. Mother has in effect re-projected back into baby a modified form of what he projected into mother and which he then introjected with a resulting modification of his personality.

The process is this: baby's crying projects feelings into mother so that she can feel and understand them for him; mother does some sophisticated sensual/emotional/intellectual operations to identify what his need is; mother puts the food into baby; through mother's act itself the baby takes in (introjects and identifies with) the capacity to understand his own feelings. This is a paradigm of the idea of emotional containing and its relation to personal development. It is exemplified in the example in the last chapter (E 18.1, 'Tackling the attendance problem') by the projections and eventually the gentler re-projections of responsibility.

The containing relationship

Bion (1970) has developed a primitive typology of containing. He describes the relationship between container and contents – the contents being the projected emotional experience. He identifies three types of this relationship.

In the first form the container overwhelms and crushes the life out of the contents. Bion uses examples which are explicitly social, and he thinks of an army encircling another, but also of an individual's genius being crushed by a particularly rigid social establishment – as in the case of Galileo, for instance. An emotional example would be the child whose feelings are constantly disconfirmed, dismissed or explained away by a mother who does not allow herself to feel properly for her child.

Another form of the relationship is one in which the contents explode the container, such as when a revolutionary person or idea blows apart the established order of society – Christ, for example, or Freud, Bion says! An emotional example would be a child whose feelings destroy mother's confidence so that she ends up shattered, depressed and completely put out of action as a mother.

Finally, in the third form, container and contents manage to accommodate to each other and in the process both develop and grow – a mother, for instance, who in spite of the agonies of feeling her child's distress can stick with it in order to project her understanding into her child for the sake of his growth, and who can therefore grow herself in the process.

This is a categorization which can be used to discriminate between therapeutic and non-therapeutic containing, including the way in which social institutions contain the individuals in them. These forms of the containing relationship can be plotted on the dimensions I described in chapter 17. Bion's container exploded by its contents corresponds to the fragmented community. The crushed contents correspond to the constriction of individuals by the rigid community dedicated to eradicating the individual's own experience. The third relationship between container and contents in which both accommodate and grow corresponds to the flexible community.

The containing community

It is perhaps quite a startling discovery of the social psychiatry movement that disturbed, deviant and anti-social people collected together under one roof erect a quite definite social entity. What that community is like may vary widely but it is, within itself, consistent and can be described and classified.

Disturbance and madness is imported into a mental health institution of some kind. There it is constrained into some sort of order. That process is a containing function. The question is, what is the quality of the containing? What kind of containing relationship is it?

If containing is some kind of externalization of individual distress into a commonly shared set of attitudes and experiences then individuals may feel strengthened by it through introjecting collective support for a defensiveness. Alternatively, they may gain through introjecting the capacity to face and understand their distress from a good (flexible) containing community. Thus, as mental health institutions vary, so the quality of containing may be better or worse.

The function of the old-fashioned mental hospital is expressed by certain symbols of containment – high walls, locked doors, official uniforms. This rigid containment of madness is not performed merely by these physical features. They are symbols of the kind of social container which it is.

Mental health institutions exist for people who cannot contain themselves – in spite of the resources of their normal social and family environment. Sometimes their environment has actively inflamed their uncontainable fears. Some people frequently feel that they cannot contain themselves. Normal society fails them. They require special intervention.

Since he is part of the process of the overhaul and adaptation of the community, and also the cause of its typical regime, the individual personality has the chance to acquire for himself a more flexible attitude to his own internal states, and a greater tolerance for his own experiences.

The typology of communities

We can ask the question, how successful is a particular institution? Defensive communities are successful at keeping the member at a distance from his own experience and, as we have seen, there are a number of kinds of such a community. The dimensions C and R, cohesiveness and rigidity, distinguish the kinds of defensive community we have come across in the illustrations. Figure 19.1 is a three-dimensional display of the four types of defensive community regime in relation to the flexible regime. In this section I shall review these types of the community with reference to the examples given in this book.

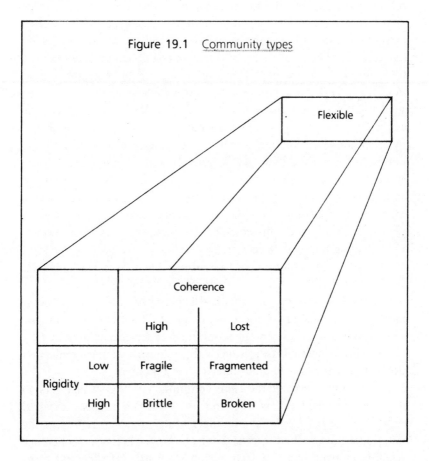

Figure 19.1   Community types

The fragile community has low rigidity and is characterized by the fear of going to pieces. Any disturbance is very threatening to stability and seems easily to provoke self-defeating group phenomena which exacerbate the threat. Typically this kind of community personality has a very short life, degenerating rapidly into fragmentation or adopting rigid strategies to shore itself up. Therefore it is only ever glimpsed. The best example is at the group level – the students in E 14.7 reached a point of sudden fragility which then went on to manifestations of both rigid clinging and splintering fragmentation. At the community level, examples E 15.1 ('The quarrelsome intruder') and E 15.2 ('The emotional intruder') show the community in a very vulnerable condition, weak and open to the effects of Ben, the quarrelsome intruder, and Brenda, the emotional intruder. Features of the demoralized community (abandonment of the task, task drift, mutual projection systems between the individual and the meeting) were on the verge of closing in. E 11.1 ('The hamstrung community') shows the community on the edge of a similar disaster. 'The Easter disruption' (E 15.3) shows a similar state from which the community managed to rescue itself and move towards the flexible state. Here the community tends to be undifferentiated, held together in a fragile way by an adhesive or clinging activity. The typical personalities are the intensely narcissistic types we described as the monologuist (E 6.3) and the silent member (E 6.4). These personalities typically establish an undifferentiated merging relationship. In contrast, we have seen a number of moments when the community fragments and goes to pieces. Typically the schizoid ruler dominates and, as in example E 15.5 ('Ruling fragmentation'), fragmentation rules.

The rigid community has two forms. When it remains cohesive, as it invariably does, there is the typical restriction on change and the determined prevention of individual experience. This type of community is dominated by the bureaucrat. E 16.1 'The bureaucratic constitution', demonstrates the numbing of experience in the constricting faceless concern. Ossification (E 16.2) shows how the organization prevents any possible dissolution even for a moment.

The other form of the rigid community is the special version described in chapter 7 as 'the iron fist' in which a strong external control is exerted by the community, which comes to represent the individuals' discredited internal controls. Nevertheless, its coherence remains vulnerable and I have termed it brittle. If the rigid community does break, it forms parts (which may be multiple), each fighting tenaciously for its own self-interest. This is the broken community (see E 7.2, 'The ruling mafiosi', and the account of the traditional mental hospital in chapter 11). The phenomenon of complexity (E 16.3) represents an organization which rigidly sticks together, but without proper integration.

The regimes and their leaders described in chapter 7 correspond to these community types – the schizoid personality in the fragmented community, the bureaucrat in the brittle community, and the psychopath in the broken community.

This typology of communities is not dry categorization for the sake of it. It dwells on the flesh and blood of human feelings and experience.

As we have seen, it is a cruel nemesis that the patient in trouble twists the community into a distorted version of what it should be. Through his misperceptions he may actually contribute to the development of a pathological organization. The member of the community makes of his one hope a replica of his own internal tragedy.

Summary

Communities contain human tensions and emotional distress. It is the job of a mental health institution to do so. Some communities seem to go to pieces in the process of trying to contain. The phantasy of the fragmented container (community) is very deep-seated in most people. The dimensions of the community personality described in chapter 17 give rise to a typology of communities as containers. This fits in easily with the observations in chapter 7 about characteristic personality types and the regimes they appear to sponsor. However much the community is a container for anxious individuals, it is only an auxiliary container for people who are not able to contain themselves.

20

Therapy in practice

I shall now consider an extended example of the community working to establish a therapeutic relationship with a patient. The patient was an anti-social psychopath. She was in the process of setting up an external agent to correspond to her characteristic internal object-relationship. The community hovered around this problem in a typical fashion. A tension is palpable between her defensive regime and a flexible accommodation to her. In the end there was some development both in the patient and in the community. I shall emphasize two aspects at the outset – leadership and containing.

Leadership: One can distinguish between two kinds of leadership. First, those which generate dramatizations and its roles. We saw this in E 4.1, 'The persecuted victim', and E 4.2, 'A mother's remorse'. In contrast to this is the leader who holds the primary task in mind and, through reflection on the experience, can try to hold both sides of the dramatized relationship together. We will discuss this 'bridging function' shortly.

Therapeutic communities are often muddled about leadership because this distinction is not made clear. There is then an inviting opening for dramatizations of anti-authority relationships. One might say that one of the prime objectives in a therapeutic community is the work of keeping the two kinds of leadership clear and separate.

Containing: A community which is therapeutic must aim for a flexible containing function. That means a mutual adaptation of both individual and community to each other. The community needs to accommodate an individual who is on the run from his own worst fears. Patients will make this need clear, often in dramatized form (see E 9.4, 'Accommodating patients'). In turn, the individual has the opportunity to accommodate a community which is accommodating to his dramatizations. The community accommodates by adapting its structure, but also in this process the problem and dramatization are put into words. Typically, both sides of what is dramatized between the patient and the community must be held together. Thus the bridging referred to above becomes a central element of the work.

The problems encountered in chapter 2 are now set in a clear framework. The task is to locate one's own experience in this framework, not merely to react to the experience.

The working therapist

To help with this work I shall offer some guidelines on practice. These depend, however, on the person's own intuition, on his capacity to hold his own immediate experience for a moment of reflection. His experience belongs to the group as well as to him privately. It is his personal door into the group arena.

A crisis in the course of one patient's membership of the community demonstrated the way in which the organization of the whole community became implicated. The structure filled with tension and changed in terms of distance and miscommunications. The anxieties and feelings of the individual coloured in the organization as a human and emotional 'organism'.

E 20.1 Therapy is a community process

The day hospital had an associated facility – accommodation for a dozen or so in-patients. This nursing facility was used extensively by the community as short-stay intensive care for members who went through severe emotional crises during their treatment. The running of the 'unit', as it was called, was rather separate from the day hospital. For example, many of the staff working at nights rarely come into contact with the whole community. The unit had for some time a very 'dependent' culture with little self-help. This was respected by the community, by and large, as a suitable provision for severe crises. Regression was accepted.

A young psychopathic girl, Gladys, succeeded in making a very considerable impact with aggressive threats and fights and with uncontrolled self-mutilating acts of cutting, drugging and drinking. Other patients in the unit were afraid of her, several nurses threatened to resign because they were being asked to look after 'unsuitable cases'. The problem grew in proportion. The community was faced with a crisis on a community scale. The whole issue came to the community meetings time and time again, but always with the air of being second-hand. Those patients involved in the unit were reluctant to speak and the night nurses were not present at these day meetings. This was all compounded by this patient's ability to confuse and distort. Gladys was not bright intellectually but, one could say, she was bright enough to use her intellectual handicap with great effect to give the impression of inexplicable and ill-defined acts taking place at uncertain times and places. As the crisis went on the early attempts to control this patient and to put conditions on her fell easily to the same fate – they were discredited as confused and ill-defined. The unit became an even further distant and poorly-understood part of the hospital.

Now, this is a central problem for a therapeutic community. The problems which arise are typical: something must be done; people may be attacked and hurt physically (as well as emotionally); staff will leave; the patient has created for herself a situation not at all to her own benefit and needs rescuing from it. She was actively creating a punitive object-relationship externalized into the community which could then be dealt with by discrediting it.

Yet the capacity for decisive action by the community was destroyed in confusion. This was a highly charged situation, as frustrations rose on all sides, and everyone felt discredited. It was a situation which would seem to provide considerable opportunity for therapeutic advantage, yet everything seemed to evaporate in confusion as soon as it was touched upon.

It was clear enough that the confusion was a motivated one. It was in the service of keeping up the distance between the community meeting, which would become for the patient the punitive agent, and the unit which was the arena for her misdemeanours. The structural division in the hospital organization became a defensive splitting operation which relieved the patient of her internal punitive object-relationship.

The structural division had become emotionally charged. Suspicions mounted to a crescendo across it indicating the formation of a barrier which was the nub of a collective system of defence.

For the nursing staff of the unit, their own impotence when faced with this unruly girl could be projected into the community meeting. For them, the community was the incompetent agent which could not assess suitable patients. On the other hand, for the community, the unit had become a repository for the madness and the fears about madness. The problems were located over there. It was the unit and the unit staff which were afraid of and defeated by madness. As in example E 14.5, 'The day community penetrated', a patient was used to accomplish the projection. Gladys lent herself admirably to the dramatization of this kind of projective inter-group relationship.

Although there was a sensible logic about allowing more disturbed patients to regress, and having an in-patient facility to admit them to at such moments in their treatment, here was an example of the way in which the procedure could be used unconsciously to effect projections. Madness was to be kept away and out of sight in this projective manner – rather like the traditional use of the traditional mental hospital.

Thus the dramatization was based on resources which derived from the features of the patient's own personality, from the organizational structure of the hospital, and from emotional fears about madness.

It was a serious problem looked at from the dynamic level. Distance was put between the community meeting and the unit in order to externalize the projections to as remote an area as possible. However, the more distance there was, the more scope this patient had to create confusion and dissension between the two parts of the organization. And the experience of the structure splitting apart at the seams reverberated within the individuals and enhanced the insecurity and fear of going to pieces. In turn, this stimulated the projection of fear of madness to as great a distance as possible. A cyclical unconscious process drove the situation, with the aim of some defensive gain, but with a constant overall deterioration of the situation.

What might the community actually do? One possibility would have been simply to discharge Gladys – an option all the members of the community considered at some point. However, there was an awareness, widespread amongst the patients and staff, that things were not quite as simple. People who became involved did so, it was realized, for their own reasons (or, more accurately for their own emotions).

What was known by the whole community at this time was that several of the nurses had for quite incidental reasons decided to leave the hospital anyway. This had resulted in a sense of insecurity for many people and it was clear that this was affecting the issue. The ability of the unit to contain uncontrollable behaviour depended on the constancy of the care by the staff. And this was threatened. The outbreak of uncontrollable behaviour was an infectious fear where so many have experienced breakdown personally. In this case, the opportunity had arisen for the fear of breakdown to be located in the unit. That is to say, for the majority of the community, this fear could at this point in time be externalized and put at a projected distance. The result offered great relief to each individual even though he then became involved in an exceedingly difficult community problem. The confusion, distortions and exaggerations allowed the community view of the situation in the unit to approach more and more closely to the private phantasies of disaster the individuals held within them.

There were other aspects to the crisis. Gladys's admission to the community and then to the unit occurred in yet another context. There had been ongoing discussion amongst the staff over the question of staff responsibility versus patient responsibility, and this led on to some disagreement about methods, criteria for suitability, and the role of nurses.

Much more was in question than the behaviour of one patient. Four factors had come together: Gladys's psychopathology; an insecurity due to staff leaving; the fear of madness at this time; and disagreements and divisions amongst the staff. The structural division of the organization was perfectly placed to draw in large quantities of emotion and disturbance through the mediating effect of this suitable patient. The deceptively localized problem was actually a congealed knot of community issues.

To return to what the community did: one aspect of the crisis was the psychological distance of the nursing unit from the community meeting. The community therefore decided to set up a meeting consisting of staff representatives, the unit patients and the night nursing staff. It was implied that staff members had the role of bridging the gulf and the confusion. And it was accepted as a legitimate staff role that they should initiate this.

The outcome of that special meeting, which the particular patient failed to attend, was that the community as a whole could now be asked to put very strict limits on this patient, and this was eventually done. There was now more confidence that the liaison with the unit over what the patient was up to would not rest solely with the patient herself. There was an explicit sanction that the patient would be discharged from the unit (though not from the day community) if she crossed the limits.

More than this, the members of the unit had come to recognize something else. In the presence of the staff accepting responsibility for making a bridge between the night nurses and the community meeting, the patients living in the unit realized that the responsibility normally lay in their hands. They actually, with staff help, began to organize for that. A nightly 'unit meeting' was arranged, which would report back to the community meeting. In spite of their especially disturbed condition, the unit patients were none the less able to recognize the responsibilities of the position they were in. They alone in the community meetings really knew what was going on in the unit.

The community meeting had been rescued from its difficulty by the unit meeting. The community had been unable to act because the unit patients used their apparently regressed state as an excuse not to aid the necessary communication process. The community itself had wished partly to remove the feared madness and insecurity beyond the horizon into some oblivion of confusion. Having begun to face this, there was a new decisiveness and in fact subsequently, when the patient transgressed some of the conditions laid down by getting drunk, the community agreed to discharge her forthwith from the unit, inviting her to continue as a day patient until she could assure the community that she would no longer drink.

Having challenged the idea of the totally regressed mad patient admitted to the unit for a spell of completely responsibility-free nursing care, the process of getting patients to accept some responsibility was initiated without it taking over the role of omnipotent external punitive controller. The patient began to have a chance of introjecting a new kind of internal control, one which was certainly strict, but also less punitive and less easy to discredit. The community, on the other hand, had faced some of the unspoken views about madness and the complete breakdown of the responsible side of their personalities. Finally, the organization itself developed in a realistic way to improve communications where needed.

To summarize this process: the structure of the organization became filled with the tensions of the members, and that was catalysed by one person in particular. The shared problems of community life at that moment were concealed, but expressed through the fate of madness and disturbance, dramatized in the inter-group arena. While there was not an adequate and sensitive recognition of the overall community tensions there was a free-wheeling progress into an increasingly intense projection system with declining communications and an uncontrollable life at the level of dramatization. However, with a growing awareness of the tensions and issues in the community as a whole, it became possible to plan a structural intervention in which an adequate bridging function could begin. The bridge was only at a superficial glance one between the unit and the community; it was really the beginning of a bridge between irresponsible madness and a fearful but 'sane' awareness.

The verbal bridge

Bringing together separated parts of the community provides a chance of bringing about internal integration of parts of the personalities of the involved members. The community is a very versatile stage for dramatizing psychological distance, and the maintenance of the community structure represents a therapeutic opportunity for the bringing-together of unintegrated parts of the members' personality. These inter-group splits and their integration exactly represent the dramatized roles seen in community meetings. The person in a role in a meeting is used exactly in the same way as the unit that was projected into, and as Gladys who was used as the projected element. These distorted identities are of great importance therapeutically in so far as they can be used also to represent the healing of identities and personalities as well as the fragmentation of them.

Turquet describes vividly the member of staff attempting to solve the problem of using his position in a dramatized role (that of the aggressor) in order to bring about some integration in the group:

> *A word of warning: because the anger ... is a projected anger, the recipient being the consultant, and because it rarely comes from one source but from many and hence has a summation quality to it, the anger in transit may be experienced as arising quite suddenly within the introjecting consultant. As part of his work, however, he will start to talk about the experience of being angry, thereby using it constructively. He may then encounter a not unusual response ... frank disbelief. This disbelief may have two further consequences. First to leave him with the anger and hence to isolate him. Secondly to fill him up further with angry reproaches: 'how can he say such a thing?', 'It must be his imagination!' or 'I get pissed off when I hear the consultants talk like that' – which serves to isolate him. To climb back, as it were, or get on top of this situation, he may have to use force, maybe by speaking loudly or emphatically, or commanding silence by his weighty entry or personal self-assertiveness; so to be told he is 'obviously angry'. Something of an impasse is reached. To be silent about such experiences originating from the group is to go under. To assert such experiences verbally is to be violent. The technical solution is the interpretation of both aspects – to go under or to survive by domination – where both aspects also reflect the members problems.* (1975, p. 129)

Turquet is describing just the same problems of making interpretations. A dramatized relationship closed in on the staff member (consultant) and trapped him into the role of an angry authority. Turquet is vivid about the problems of trying to regain some authority. His efforts only led him deeper into the dramatization, and he became more and more trapped in the role he was trying to get out of.

His technical solution – the interpretation of both aspects – is correct because it relates, as he says, to the whole experience of the members. To try to talk about his own angry experience did no better than to assert his own authority. The bridging function can be achieved in the meeting by using words to span the two aspects of the experience – the dominating aggressor, and the defeated one who goes under.

The meeting can reinterpret one's efforts so fast that it is hard to keep one's head. Yet if one can, it brings about the most revealing moment of all.

In the example we have just considered it was the structure of the whole organization that came to be reinterpreted. The psychological distance which crept into the fracture lines of the organization as a barrier needed just the same bridging. It was carried out in structural adaptation as well as in words. It could not be done without words and a conscious recognition of the two sides of the barrier.

Summary

This chapter has described the problems posed to the community when a structural distance between parts of the community came to be exploited for the emotional distancing of split-off experiences. Although the problem congealed around one partiuclar patient, problematic experiences were sucked in from various sources within the community. The example described the therapeutic bridging of this structural, architectural and emotional distance. It is claimed that the bridging function is a core element in the therapeutic management of the community and is central to the movement of the community along dimension F towards a flexible regime.

21

Guidelines for the staff

At the beginning of this book I emphasized the importance of the individual's own experience, and that this was the working tool of the staff member of a therapeutic community. We are now in a position to determine how to work with this instrument. It is most straightforward, perhaps, to formulate under three basic principles certain questions that a member of staff should ask of himself as he works in the community. I will then go on to ask these questions from the point of view of a day staff member in the community meeting in E 20.1.

1. A member of staff must try to remain familiar with his own experience of the moment. He should observe the following:
   - (a) Does he feel he is being sucked into something emotional which traps him or makes him feel disconfirmed?
   - (b) Does he feel that he is in a particular emotional position in the group?
   - (c) Can he experience the emotional position of the other aspect of the group experience?

2. This leads to the staff member reflecting on his experience of his feelings of the moment and the position which puts him into the group. He should then check his perceptions:

    (a)   What other roles in the dramatization can he see?

    (b)   Does he find an impulse to respond to someone at the individual level only?

    (c)   Who are the leaders of what is going on?

    (d)   Are they leaders of a community dramatization, or of a bridge across a barrier?

3. At this point the member of staff may be in a position to make an intervention. This could be simply to ask a question or prompt further activity. It may, however, be to venture an interpretation which would start to try to bridge the emotional distances. He may wish to come in to support someone else's efforts to start a bridge. Whatever he does, he then has to watch the response.

    (a)   Has the intervention been taken as he intended? – or has it sucked him into a dramatization (back to question 1(a))?

    (b)   If there is no immediate response, how does he experience the silence? – does he feel it is being reflected upon, or does the silence put him into a position he had not expected to feel?

    (c)   Or if it was somebody else who made an intervention, how does he feel himself about that intervention?

    (d)   And how has that person fared?

The staff member

We can now imagine the position of someone in the community meeting in E 20.1 when it was at the height of its problem. Let us call him Dave.

1(a) Sucked into something?

Being present at the community meeting was a frustrating business. It all seemed so unclear. Dave could not make up his mind about what was going on over there in the 'unit'. They seemed to be pretty irresponsible, not getting anything organized, and they didn't seem to know if they were coming or going. They were being irresponsible. Gladys was so unreasonable. She was a troublemaker. A proper eye should be kept on her, but how could that be done by the day community when she went and got drunk at night.

1(b) Dave's own emotional position in the group?

Dave felt it was impossible. He wondered how the other staff were feeling. It seemed the staff were supposed to do something, but all he could do was feel useless. The staff in the 'unit' should be doing a lot more to put their problem patients back into line and not bother the community with these issues. Why did he get so frustrated with all this? Perhaps he was tired after his row last night with his girlfriend in the pub. But perhaps he was being put on the spot by being in an impossible position to help out the unit when they couldn't get things clear (it felt a bit like his girlfriend!). What did it mean, feeling they were being put on the spot by the nightstaff in the 'unit'?

1(c) The other's emotional position?

The patient should probably never have been admitted – it was only because Tess was new here and wanted to prove what she can do with a patient like this. Dave wondered why his condemnation and dismissive rejection had turned on Tess as well. He wondered if these denigrating views of his colleagues were valid or distorted. Did the night staff feel at a loss too? And what were they thinking of Dave and the rest in the community meeting? Perhaps they felt high and dry too. Dave supposed that there was a big gulf between them. Perhaps that was important if the community and the 'unit' were so stretched apart, a kind of divorce really. Perhaps a lot of people were feeling powerless and some, like Tess, wanted to prove themselves (like Dave with his girlfriend).

2(a) What other roles are in the dramatization?

The night nurses were getting a lot of stick from Gladys – that was clear to see; and also from the day members as well. Dave began to perceive something. Gladys was making monkeys out of them, running them round in circles, so that they looked like fools rather than caring professionals and sensible authorities trying to keep minimal order. Gladys was playing the victim of oppression in the unit.

Which was right? Was she oppressed by unreasonable retaliation? Or was she the secret victor by virtue of making fools of them? Then there was Tess – she kept pushing the meeting. It was as if Tess was using Gladys to prove something. She was anxious to get something sorted out, but she wanted the community to do what the unit had to do at night. It seemed like something kept getting acted out in various places – something to do with being powerless and making someone else (somewhere else) feel it. It kept getting split off and shoved away somewhere.

2(b) Emphasizing the individual?

Dave wanted Gladys properly controlled. She seemed obviously to be the culprit. He began to feel a sympathy for the nurses in the 'unit' again. Once she was dealt with he would feel that the problem was solved. And he wanted a meeting which would tell Gladys to behave herself in the unit and stop drinking.

2(c) The leading individuals?

Gladys was central to the problem. But she didn't seem to lead except by provoking. Then there was Tess, the person who wanted her admitted, who wanted the community to get on and do something. Then there was Veronica, another member of staff, who wanted the unit to be involved in these discussions – but how could you expect the night staff to come to these meetings? He supposed that Gladys was leading this process of making staff powerless and discrediting them. Veronica seemed to be leading something else – she wasn't trying to prove anything.

2(d) Dramatizations or bridges?

Perhaps, in wanting to set up discussions with the night nurses, Veronica was doing something different from the others. She seemed to feel sure of herself and wasn't knocked off balance by the hectoring she was coming under from Gladys. She kept saying that the night nurses must have a point of view to express. Dave had thought that too. Maybe she was trying to link (make a bridge between) the foolish nurses who didn't seem to know what they were doing with the rest of us who were criticizing them.

3(a) Response to an intervention?

When Tess had said that Gladys should be stopped from going out in order to stop her drinking Dave had added his opinion to emphasize her words. He had said that Gladys should listen to Tess. Such a straightforward arrangement would get it all sorted out quickly. But somehow Gladys had twisted his meaning by bringing in that occasion when he had met her in a pub by chance, and had brought her a drink (his girlfriend had got cross, thinking he was being too nice to Gladys). And then Tess had seemed cross when this came up, and he felt he must have undermined her by his comment but he couldn't understand how. Dave thought about it, and it seemed he was part of the same thing. He had jumped in wanting to control Gladys but had ended up looking a bit foolish and over involved – like an amateur.

3(b) What kind of silence?

Later on he asked Veronica how the night staff might be able to come to the meeting, and there was a long silence. He felt uncomfortable at first, but she looked round the room as if she thought people ought to take that question seriously. Someone eventually said that he and Veronica ought to go to the unit one evening as special representatives of the day community. He could feel then that some shift had taken place. It seemed as though a different kind of action had unfolded, one which wasn't designed to manipulate, to make people feel something, and enact roles.

3(c) Someone else's intervention?

When Tess had been trying to persuade Gladys, he had felt she was being too easy-going, so he had wanted to toughen the meeting up. He began to realize how he wanted Gladys punished. Tess had become more and more anxious as she pushed Gladys harder and harder. It was as if she had started something she could not stop. It also seemed to revolve around someone being very strict to someone else and being defeated, or else trying to care for them and being made a fool of. Until Veronica had started the new tack.

3(d) The fate of the intervener?

Veronica kept coming back to her point about bringing the night nurses into the discussion. At first her remarks were ignored, but after Tess had got caught up in haggling with Gladys, Will had said he didn't know whether the 'unit' was supposed to punish or to care for people. Dave thought it was a good point, because there seemed to be discussion going on from both points of view. Then Veronica asked how we could discuss that without the staff from the unit. And this time he had come in on her side because it seemed so sensible – and after someone had thought of sending representatives, they had set up the new meeting in the unit. Dave felt a bit pleased, but he also felt that he'd been given a mighty big job to handle.

The ability to work in this way depends on the person's own intuition, and on his capacity to hold his own immediate experience for a moment of reflection. His experience belongs to the group as well as to him privately. It is his personal door into the group arena.

Summary

I have presented guidelines to focus the use of personal capacities for intuition and reflection. These guidelines can be reduced to a small set of questions which should be held on to as continual indicators in the minds of therapeutic community workers.

The first question: *Is this the dramatization of some unconscious object-relationship?* It is important to check whether some unrealistic emotional relationship is being played out between individuals in the meeting.

The second question: *Am I being sucked into a role in some dramatization?* The activity in the meetings and groups and the inter-group relations may be expressing some collective defensiveness. Experiencing oneself involved in suspicions and hostilities should be checked and verbalized. Sides should not be taken.

The third question: *Why is this particular person assigned to this particular role in the dramatization? And what does it say about his own personality?* The individual's valency for a role is very important. The relationship he is involved in externally in the community is important for him internally in his own phantasy. It is therapeutically important for him to link up these separated parts of his personality again.

The fourth question: *Is there a temptation to focus on one troublesome patient?* Therapizing the individual is itself a dramatization (see chapter 9). It is a part of community dynamics, and should be pointed out whenever it is taking place. The individual in all his problematic glory belongs to the group.

The fifth question: *What has been the response to the last attempt to verbalize the issue?* The response to interventions is extremely revealing. The interventions themselves will indicate whether the intervener has been sucked into the dramatization. Conversely, the response will indicate whether the important therapeutic shift towards verbalization has taken place. If the intervention is sucked into the dramatization, it may mean that it was misguided.

PART VI

The group as community

22

Cross-fertilization

When they started working with small therapy groups, Bion and Foulkes transposed psychoanalytic ideas – notably *the unconscious* and *defence mechanisms*. Then when Bion reversed his interest from the small group back to psychoanalysis again he took with him the ideas of linking and containing that he had developed in his notion of the pairing culture of a group. With these ideas he was able to advance psychoanalysis through the understanding of the experiences that psychotic patients endure.

The movement from one psychotherapeutic setting to another is potentially enriching for the whole field of the psychodynamic understanding of people. I shall close this description of the therapeutic community with an account of small group therapy that can now be enriched by cross-fertilization from the perspective of the large group and the community.

To do this I shall take the main elements of the theme in this book, one by one, and relate them to small group therapy practice. In this way this chapter is therefore a summary of the whole book as well. The interrelation of the various ideas coming out of this study are set out in diagram form in Figure 22.1.

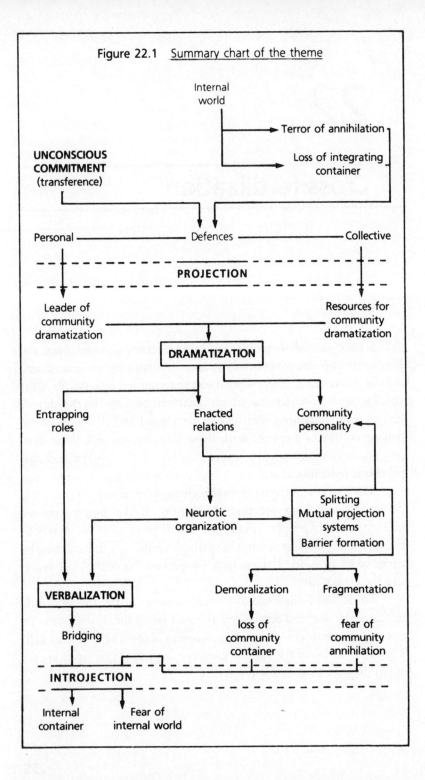

Figure 22.1   Summary chart of the theme

Internal world and projection

Each individual brings with him to any organization his own internal world of conflicts and relations. No group whatever its size is actually more than the integration of the various internal worlds which make it up. In so far as the whole of the group is more than the sum of its parts, the more is the process of integration of the individuals. The internal life of the individual is driven by love and hate and is especially spurred on by the twin fears of annihilation of the person or of his loved object. In the case of the therapeutic setting it is the rescuing quality of the therapeutic agent – therapist, group or community – which represents the good, loved object.

In connection with these fears the individual brings his own defence mechanisms, which in the life of either the community or the group become collective defences organized within the culture of the group. Central amongst these defence mechanisms is *projection*. Through this mechanism the roles in the group are assigned with insistent power, and with a resistance to realistic appreciation. The power, even of a small group, to locate an individual in a role which he has the resources to fit is phenomenal, just as community projections are enough to wreck the pursuit of the task of the organization.

Dramatizations

Because a community must maintain an active organization, and not merely a verbal discourse, the variety and intensity of the unconscious relating between individuals becomes much more visible. What the members of the group and the group therapist all bring to the group, because they are all human, is a perception of relationships between objects. It is these relationships played out within the group, between phantastical figures perceived in the group or in relation to the group and its members, which should be the first focus. And it is important to recognize that these relationships are played out as unconscious dramas, even in small therapy groups which restrict themselves simply to verbal communication. Non-verbal communications, and the phantasying activity, all have to do with very active manipulation of self and others into roles and into interpersonal positions within the group. This active mode I have termed *dramatization*, in contrast to the *verbal* expression of feelings and phantasies.

Dramatization structures a group in precise ways which are there to be noticed, and eventually described verbally for therapeutic purposes. It is as precise and as inevitable as the structure of an organization into rational or unconscious sub-groupings. In contrast to this, group therapy based on the *group-as-whole* notion (Foulkes, 1964), may degenerate into an insistence on the homogeneity of the group (de Mare, 1985). The idea of a group, as somehow above and beyond the actual reality, is a construct of the therapist, and becomes a convenient fiction for disregarding latent or disguised hostilities, especially towards the therapist. It is important to remember that the group-as-a-whole does not necessarily correspond to the perception of the group members.

Internal object-relations and community personality

The object-relations played out unconsciously in a group are visible through perceptions with the intuitive 'third eye', as it were, which records the emotional undercurrents going on within the overt interactions and in the 'space between the words'. Where do these relationships come from? A group has a deep reservoir of resources for these object-relationships in the personalities of the individuals, which contain within them a large number of unconscious phantasy relationships. These are internal relationships, like the one described by Freud between the ego and the super-ego (Freud, 1923). This comprises an internal interaction between parts of the personality, which have internal results experienced by the person as comforting or persecuting. Work in groups of all kinds, especially large groups, shows that these kinds of relationships are extremely varied, and confirms Klein's expansion of Freud's theory of internal relationships (Klein, 1929).

Freud showed that in some cases relations within the self are externalized in order to reduce the pain of these relations with the self – especially punitive relations (Freud, 1916). He was describing certain criminals who are tortured internally by a sense of guilt which is alleviated by externalizing it into a piece of actual wrongdoing that results in actual external punishment. It seems that the external punishment is never as bad as the internal phantasizing and worrying about punishment. It is often recognized that to leave a person alone with his own conscience may be much worse than prescribing an actual punishment.

This kind of externalization was therefore a defence, since it mitigated psychic pain. This was also expanded by Klein, who showed that the same process is involved in the child's externalization of his phantasies into play with toys and dolls (Klein, 1927). My contention is that this can be further extended to groups. The dramatized relationships in groups are externalizations of internal object-relations. This contention, which is set out in chapter 5, derives from Jaques (1955) who first described institutions in this way.

Community personality and the defensive culture

An organization that receives the externalizations of internal object-relationships functions as a support to the psychological defences of its individual members. The kinds of relationships that are set up, or the reactions against them, may lead to the whole organization working in a particular way such as to enhance that defensiveness. This becomes *a social defence system* of mutual projections between sub-groupings and barrier formation, and may lead to grave distortions of the actual and realistic task of the organization.

The dominant individuals, more forceful in the externalizations of their own internal worlds, colour in the community and its organization in their own image. The fit between the individual's own characteristic defences and the need of the community to deal with its current issues by means of evasions, leads to specific regimes of the community which, like the individual, can therefore be said to have a community personality.

The therapy group, attempting to operate analytically, must attend to the defensive properties of the group culture as well as those of the individuals. Indeed, many writers on group therapy regard the diversion of the group into maladaptive cultures as *the* feature of the group to focus on.

In this respect we can think of Bion's early observations (1961) where he described three group cultures, each suffused with an unspoken *basic assumption* – (i) the group is dependent on the leader (basic assumption dependency, BaD); (ii) the group has an enemy to fight or flee from (basic assumption fight/flight, BaF); and (iii) the group, in the intercourse between two or more members, is about to give birth to a Messianic idea or person (basic assumption pairing, BaP). Bion contrasted these basic assumption cultures with the *work group* culture, which is dominated by the explicit and conscious task of the group; the group has to struggle towards the work task in the teeth of being dragged back into primitive group behaviour dominated by the basic assumptions.

Ezriel (1956), in researching the psychoanalytic interpretation as a formal scientific experiment, similarly looked at group therapy in terms of the culture of the group-as-whole. Particularly in Ezriel's formulation, the defensive culture is conceived of in terms of the characteristic relationship. The culture of the group is only a surface manifestation, a *required relationship*; and it is required because there is a hidden relationship that has to be avoided, the *avoided relationship*, which in turn is avoided because it will lead to a *calamity*. In Ezriel's view the culture of the group is a complex manifold of relationships resembling the psychoanalytic conflict between unconscious urges and defensive avoidance.

Similar to this structure of relationships is the distinction made by Whitaker and Lieberman (1964) between *restrictive solutions* and *enabling solutions*. In their view the group, faced with a group issue of some kind (the *group focal conflict*), has a choice of solutions; the easiest, usually evasive, is the *restrictive solution* (see E 9.1, 'Therapizing the individual'), which leads to a maladaptive group culture; alternatively, the *enabling solution*, usually to be struggled for by the group, allows free expression and wider options for the group members.

The interaction of the individual defensiveness and the organizational defensiveness is a complex one which involves unconscious negotiation of the leadership at any one time. This is a negotiation over whose internal relations shall be adopted for externalization, which depends also on the group issues and the fit between the individuals' own defensiveness and their suitability for the major elements of the group. Thus the regime in the group is an integration of the group issues and the particular resources within the individuals for externalization of appropriate characteristic object-relationships.

Barriers and sub-grouping

The externalization of internal relationships entails establishing in the external group the same sorts of internal splitting which goes on inside the personalities of the individuals. Jaques pointed out that, in an organization, externalization such as this shows up in the distortion or blocking of communication between certain parts of the organization. The sites where these blocks and distortions occur are communication *barriers*, and indicate phantasies of the other group based on unrealistic projections across the barrier. On each side the individuals misperceive those on the other side, and do so for defensive purposes. The defensive culture of one sub-grouping depends on the misperceptions of themselves and the counter-perception of the other sub-group.

Alliances within the small group carry the same sort of projective forces as the communication barriers in an organization. They are forces sustained by the group attention being distracted from them, and are a clue to the central issues of the group, its defensiveness and the uncontained anxieties being evaded. In addition, even in small out-patient groups, the existence of others, individuals or groups, outside the group is often extremely important, even if it is only a *phantasy* about another group. It is often on the unspoken references to other groups that the culture is maintained.

Roles and scapegoats

The barriers which mark off a sub-group that is used for defensive projections may mark off the smallest of all groups, the individual himself. In that case a person carries a particular role in which he is separate from the rest of the group in unspecified but crucial ways. The unconscious defensiveness entails projecting certain characteristics into him and relating to him with the characteristic internal object-relationships. This assigned role is intended to deal with a community issue affecting the major element of the group, and is a response to the unconscious aspects of the individual's own personality that fit the particular scapegoat role needed at the time. With great pressure of anxiety from the community issues, these roles imprison even the most reluctant participants.

261

Demoralization and fragmentation

Like the neurotic defences of the individual, a group that adopts a defensive culture and enacts dramatizations as the foremost part of its activity will tend to spoil its own effectiveness for achieving its stated purpose. The creation of barriers and the declining quality of communications within result in an increasingly tense organization which then deals with the increased tension by further moves into a defensive culture. Further sub-grouping, with barrier-formation and thus increasing fragmentation, gives rise to lower morale and yet further defensiveness.

In small groups where the purpose of the group is to come together in a way that is therapeutic, the task will become distorted and drift into omnipotent or shallow efforts to make everyone better. Since most members of a small therapeutic group will be completely unfamiliar with what is required, the ensuing bewilderment and sense of despair within is frequently dealt with by means of the formation of defensive cultures – such as *therapizing* the individual, where the barrier forms around a single individual, and a relationship (group to individual) dramatizes a defensive hoping-for-the-best effort that is inevitably sterile.

Just like the community that is fragile in its organization, a small group can fall apart into fragments. Overt forms of dispersion that wreck the small groups – absenteeism, dropping-out, and a characteristic form of retreat by the individuals into a mutism and silent phantasizing while the group is in progress – are common evidence of *dramatizations of fragmentation*. Individual withdrawals, in a physical sense or a psychological one, render even a small group psychologically fragmented. The reverberation between internalizations and externalizations on which the belonging to the group depends brings about mounting fears in the individual, in identification with his group, that he too is fragmenting.

Flexibility, containing and internalization

Not all organizations get stuck in the vicious circle of the demoralization trap. The key to whether or not an organization can find its way out is whether the individuals' anxieties contained in the organization are *rigidly* or *flexibly* dealt with. The rigid regime has been described as involving projection across barriers with declining communication and increasing fragmentation of the organization and the individuals.

In contrast, a flexible organization demonstrates the opposite features – the ability to test the veracity of perceptions of others without sticking to discredited projected stereotypes, the maintenance of the control of communication quality, and the sustaining of a realistic sense of purpose and task.

This is a dimension – from the rigid to the flexible – which is apparent in all human interactions. And in small group therapy the issue is how to move a group of defensive individuals who have an investment in creating a rigid defensive culture in support of their own individual defences, towards a group that sustains a more flexible regime. Ultimately the only therapeutic effect of a group (or any therapy) is the eventual internalization back into the individuals of some more flexible features derived from the group.

At the outset the contrast was made between the dramatizing mode and the verbalizing one. The key to the flexibility which needs to be on offer from the group for the individual to introject it in the course of his identification and belonging with the group, lies in the ability to sustain a verbal expression of all the issues.

However, it is not simply any verbal expression that is required, but an expression of the relationships engaged in across barriers. This is a verbal *bridging* function, an act that can encompass in one sentence uttered by one individual both sides of the dramatized relationships going on between individuals or between sub-groups, or between individual and group.

Bion remarked that no person exists except in relation to a group, and that this 'valency' consists of: 'characteristics in the individual whose real significance cannot be understood unless it is realized that they are part of his equipment as a herd animal and their operation cannot be seen unless it is looked for in the intelligible field of study – which in this instance is the group. You cannot understand a recluse living in isolation unless you inform yourself about the group of which he is a member' (Bion, 1961, p. 133). In the same way no group exists without having the equipment for being a community and contributing to a system of sub-groups within a community. In this sense, the group and its individual cannot be understood unless the pieces of equipment for life as a community – especially *dramatizations*, *barriers* and *bridging* – are looked for.

Bibliography

All books are published in London unless otherwise indicated.

Adler, G. (1972) 'Helplessness in the helpers', *Br. J. Med. Psychol.* 45:315–26.

Anzieu, D. (1984) *The Group and the Unconscious*. Routledge & Kegan Paul.

Asch, S.E. (1952) *Social Psychology*. New Jersey: Prentice-Hall.

Baron, C. (1984) 'The Paddington Day Hospital: crisis and control in a therapeutic institution', *International Journal of Therapeutic Communities* 5:157–70.

—— (1987) *Asylum to Anarchy*. Free Association Books.

Barton, R. (1959) *Institutional Neurosis*. Bristol: Wright & Sons.

Bateson, G., Jackson, D.D., Haley, J. and Weakland, J. (1956) 'Toward a theory of schizophrenia', *Behavoural Science* 1:251–64.

Berke, J.H. (1982) 'The Arbours Crisis Centre', *International Journal of Therapeutic Communities* 3:248–61.

Bion, W.R. (1961) *Experience in Groups*. Tavistock.

—— (1970) *Attention and Interpretation*. Tavistock.

Bott, E. (1976) 'Hospital and society'. *Br. J. Med. Psychol.* 19:97.

Christian, A.S. and Hinshelwood, R.D. (1979) 'Work groups', in Hinshelwood and Manning (1979).

Clark, D. (1964) *Administrative Therapy*. Tavistock.

Clemental-Jones, C. (1985) 'The rapist: harmful strategies used by therapists and staff members in therapeutic communities', *International Journal of Therapeutic Communities* 6:7–13.

Cooper, D. (1967) *Psychiatry and Anti-Psychiatry*. Tavistock.

Crocket, R. (1966) 'Authority and permissiveness in the psychotherapeutic community: theoretical perspectives', *Am. J. Psychother.* 20:669–76.

Ezriel, H. (1956) 'Experimentation within the psychoanalytic setting', *British Journal for the Philosophy of Science* 7:29–48.

Festinger, L. (1950) 'Informal Social Communication', *Psychological Review* 57:271–82.

Festinger, L., **Schachter**, S. and **Back**, K. (1950) *Social Pressures in Informal Groups*. New York: Harper & Row.

Foster, A. (1979) 'The management of boundary crossing', in Hinshelwood and Manning (1979).

Foulkes, S. (1964) *Therapeutic Group Analysis*. George Allen & Unwin.

Freud, S. (1913) *Totem and Taboo*, in James Strachey, ed. *The Standard Edition of the Complete Psychological Works of Sigmund Freud*, 24 vols. Hogarth 1953–73. vol. 13, pp. 1–164.

———— (1914) 'Remembering, repeating and working-through'. *S.E.* 12, pp. 145–56.

———— (1916) 'Some character types met with in psychoanalytic work: criminals from a sense of guilt', *S.E.* 14, pp. 332–6.

———— (1921) *Group Psychology and the Analysis of the Ego. S.E.* 18, pp. 67–144.

———— (1923) *The Ego and the Id. S.E.* 19, pp. 1–68.

Glaser, F. (1977) 'The origins of the drug-free therapeutic community – a retrospective history', in P. Vamos and J.E. Brown, eds *Proceeedings of the Second World Conference of Therapeutic Communities*. Montreal: Portage Press.

Goffman, I. (1961) *Asylums*. Penguin.

Greene, L. (1982) 'Personal boundary management and social structure', in Pines and Raphaelson (1982).

Greene, L. and **Johnson**, D.R. (1987) 'Leadership and the structuring of the large group', *International Journal of Therapeutic Communities* 8: 99–108.

Grunberg, S.R. (1973) 'The therapeutic community and its politics', *Association of Therapeutic Communities Newsletter* 7.

Gunn, J., **Robertson**, G., **Dell**, S. and **Way**, C. (1978) *Psychiatric Aspects of Imprisonment*. Academic Press.

Guntrip, H. (1961) *Schizoid Phenomena, Object Relations and the Self*. Hogarth.

Higgin, G. and **Bridger**, J. (1965) 'The Psychodynamics of an Inter-group Experience', *Tavistock Pamphlet* 10.

Hinshelwood, R.D. (1972) 'A treatment model for a community', *Association of Therapeutic Communities Newsletter* 6.

—— (1979) 'Demoralisation in the hospital community', *Group-Analysis* XII: 84–93.

—— (1980) 'The seeds of disaster', *International Journal of Therapeutic Communities* 1:181–8.

—— (1982) 'Complaints against the community meeting', *International Journal of Therapeutic Communites* 3:88–94.

—— (1983) 'Projective identification and Marx's concept of man', *Int. Rev. Psycho-Anal.* 10:221–5.

—— (1983a) 'Editorial: our three-way see-saw', *International Journal of Therapeutic Communities* 4:167–8.

—— (1985) 'Anti-therapeutic forms of cohesiveness in groups', *International Journal of Therapeutic Communities* 6:133–42.

—— (1986) 'Britain and the psychoanalytic tradition in therapeutic communities', in G. de Leon and J.T. Ziegenfuss (1986).

Hinshelwood, R.D. and **Foster**, A. (1978) 'The Marlborough experiment', in J. Abercrombie, ed. *Students in Need*. Guildford: Society for Research into Higher Education.

Hinshelwood, R.D. and **Grunberg**, S.R. (1975) 'The large group syndrome', *Group-Analysis* VII. Reprinted in Hinshelwood and Manning (1979).

Hinshelwood, R.D. and **Manning**, N.P., eds (1979) *Therapeutic Communities: Reflections and Progress*. Routledge & Kegan Paul.

Hood, S. (1985) 'Staff needs, staff organisation and effective primary task performance in the residential setting', *International Journal of Therapeutic Communities* 6:15–36.

Jaques, E. (1951) *The Changing Culture of a Factory*. Routledge & Kegan Paul.

—— (1955) 'Social systems as a defence against persecutory and depressive anxiety', in M. Klein *et al.*, eds *New Directions in Psychoanalysis*. Tavistock.

de Jong, A.J. (1983) 'Eating and weight disturbance in a psychotherapy community', *International Journal of Therapeutic Communities* 4: 220–33.

Jones, M. (1982) *The Process of Change*. Routledge & Kegan Paul.

Jung, C. (1916) *The Psychology of the Unconscious*. Retitled *Symbols of Transformation*, in H. Read, M. Fordham, G. Adler and W. McGuire, eds *The Collected Works of C.G. Jung*, 20 vols. Routledge & Kegan Paul, 1951. vol. 5.

van Kalsbeck, A.G. (1980) 'The Zuideroord Story', *International Journal of Therapeutic Communities* 1:189–201.

Kennard, D. (1983) *Introduction to Therapeutic Communities* Routledge & Kegan Paul.

Kernberg, O (1984) 'The couch at sea', *Int. J. Group Psychother.* 34:5–23.

Kesey, K. (1962) *'One Flew Over the Cuckoo's Nest*. New York: Viking.

Khaleelee, O. and Miller, E. (1985) 'Beyond the small group: society as an intelligible field of study', in M. Pines (1985).

Klein, M. (1927) 'Criminal tendencies in normal children', in *The Writings of Melanie Klein*, vol. 1, pp. 170–85. Hogarth (1975).

—— (1929) 'Personification in the play of children', in *The Writings of Melanie Klein*, vol. 1, pp. 199–209.

—— (1946) 'Notes on some schizoid mechanisms', in *The Writings of Melanie Klein*, vol. 3, pp. 1–24.

Klein, R. (1981) 'The patient-staff community meeting: a tea party with the mad hatter', *Int. J. Group Psychother.* 31:205–20.

Klein, R. and Brown, S-L. (1987) 'Size and structure as variables in patient-staff community meetings', *International Journal of Therapeutic Communities* 8: 85–98.

Kreeger, L., ed. (1975) *The Large Group*. Constable.

Laing, R.D. (1960) *The Divided Self*. Tavistock.

van den Langenberg, S. and de Natris, P. (1985) 'A narrow escape from the magic mountain?', *International Journal of Therapeutic Communities* 6:91–101.

de Leon, G. and Ziegenfuss, J.T., eds (1986) *Therapeutic Communities for Addictions: Readings in Theory, Research and Practice*. Springfield, Illinois: Charles C. Thomas.

Mahler, M., Pine, F. and Bergman, A. (1975) *The Psychological Birth of the Human Infant*. Hutchinson.

Main, T.F. (1975) 'Some dynamics of large groups', in L. Kreeger (1975).

—— (1977) 'The concept of the therapeutic community: variations and vicissitudes', *Group-Analysis* X. Reprinted in Pines (1983).

Manning, N.P. (1976) 'Values and practice in the therapeutic community', *Human Relations* 29:125–8.

—— (1979) 'The politics of survival: the role of research in the therapeutic community', in Hinshelwood and Manning (1979).

—— (1980) 'Collective disturbance in institutions: a sociological view of crisis and collapse', *International Journal of Therapeutic Communities* 1:147–58.

de Mare, P.B. (1985) 'Large group perspectives', *Group-Analysis* XVIII:79–92.

Mayo, E. (1933) *The Human Problems of an Industrial Civilisation*. Boston: Harvard Business School.

McKeganey, N.P. (1986) 'Accomplishing ideals: the case of hospital-based therapeutic communities', *International Journal of Therapeutic Communities* 7:85–100.

Mendizabal de Cleriga, M. (1985) 'Oscillation in a therapeutic community', *International Journal of Therapeutic Communities* 6:37–44.

Menzies, I.E.P. (1960) 'A case study in the functioning of a social system as a defence against anxiety', *Human Relations* 13:95–121. Reprinted as *Tavistock Pamphlet* 3 (1970).

—— (1979) 'Staff support systems: task and anti-task in adolescent institutions', in Hinshelwood and Manning (1979).

Milgram, S. (1963) 'Group pressure and action against a person', *Journal of Abnormal and Social Psychology* 67:371–8.

Millard, D.W. (1986) 'Editorial: explanation in group care', *International Journal of Therapeutic Communities* 7:145–51.

Miller, E.J. and **Gwynne**, G.V. (1972) *A Life Apart*. Tavistock.

Oskarsson, H. and **Klein**, R. (1982) 'Leadership change and organisational regression', *Int. J. Group Psychother.* 32:145–62.

Pines, M., ed. (1983) *The Evolution of Group-Analysis*. Routledge & Kegan Paul.

—— (1985)*Bion and Group Psychotherapy*. Routledge & Kegan Paul.

Pines, M. and **Raphaelson**, L., eds (1982) *The Individual and the Group: Boundaries and Interrelations*. Plenum.

Ploeger, A. (1981) 'Psychodrama in an in-patient clinic', *International Journal of Therapeutic Communities* 2:13–17.

Postle, D. (1980) *Catastrophe Theory*. Fontana.

Rapoport, R.N. (1956) 'Oscillations and sociotherapy', *Human Relations* 9:357.

———— (1960) *The Community as Doctor*. Tavistock.

Rice, A.K. (1963) *The Enterprise and its Environment*. Tavistock.

Roberts, J. (1980) 'Destructive processes in groups', *International Journal of Therapeutic Communities* 1:159–70.

Rose, M. (1982) 'The potential of fantasy and the role of charismatic leadership in a therapeutic community', *International Journal of Therapeutic Communities* 3:79–87.

Rosenberg, S.D. (1970) 'Hospital culture as collective defence', *Psychiatry* 33:21–35.

Rosenfeld, H. (1971) 'A clinical approach to the psychoanalytic theory of the life and death instincts: an investigation into the aggressive aspects of narcissism', *Int. J. Psycho-Anal.* 52:169–77.

Savalle, H. and Wagenborg, H. (1980) 'Oscillations in a therapeutic community', *International Journal of Therapeutic Communities* 1:137–46.

Schlunke, J.M. and Garnett, M.H. (1986) 'Ideal, structure and defence in a small therapeutic community', *International Journal of Therapeutic Communities* 5:38–46.

Segal, H. (1973) *Introduction to the Work of Melanie Klein*. Hogarth.

Sharp, V. (1976) *Social Control in the Therapeutic Community*. Farnborough: Saxon House.

Shenker, B. (1986) *Intentional Communities*. Routledge & Kegan Paul.

Sherif, M. and Sherif, C.W. (1961) *Intergroup Conflict and Co-operation: The Robbers Cave Experiment*. Oklahoma: Institute of Group Relations.

Springman, R. (1976) 'Fragmentation as a defence in large groups', *Contemporary Psychoanalysis* 12:203.

Stanton, A and Schwartz, M. (1954) *The Mental Hospital*. New York: Basic.

Stockwell, R., Powell, A. and Bhat, A. (1986) 'Living in a therapeutic milieu: the patient's viewpoint', *International Journal of Therapeutic Communities* 7:101–9.

Sugarman, B. (1974) *Daytop Village – A Therapeutic Community*.
New York: Holt, Rinehart & Winston.
Swenson, C. (1986) 'Modification of destructiveness in the long-
term inpatient treatment of severe personality disorders',
International Journal of Therapeutic Communities 7:153–63.
Tollinton, H.J. (1969) 'The organisation of a psychotherapeutic
community', *Br. J. Med. Psychol.* 42:431.
Turquet, P. (1975) 'Threats to identify in the large group', in
Kreeger (1975).
Whitaker, D.S. and **Lieberman**, M.A. (1964) *Psychotherapy
through the Group Process*. Chicago: Aldine.
Whiteley, J.S. (1972) *Dealing with Deviants*. Hogarth.
Winnicott, D.W. (1960) 'The theory of the parent-infant
relationship', in D.W. Winnicott (1965) *The Maturational Processes
and the Facilitating Environment*. Hogarth.

Index